# NO MEAN CITY

# NO MEAN CITY:

## BELFAST 1880~1914

*in the photographs of Robert French*

'I was born in Belfast
and brought up to believe that, like St Paul,
I am a citizen of no mean city'
—George Birmingham, *Pleasant places* (London, 1934) p.1.

# Brian M. Walker and Hugh Dixon

THE FRIAR'S BUSH PRESS

For Olenka and Jill

The Friar's Bush Press
24 College Park Avenue
Belfast 7
Published 1983
© Copyright reserved.
ISBN 0 946872 00 7

The generous assistance of the Esme Mitchell Trust
and the Institute of Irish Studies, Q.U.B., is gratefully acknowledged.

Book design—Spring Graphics
Typesetting—Compuset, Belfast
Halftone reproduction—Reprographics Belfast
Printing—Manley Printing.
Binding—Q.U.B. Bindery

# CONTENTS

Donegall Place, *c.*1906

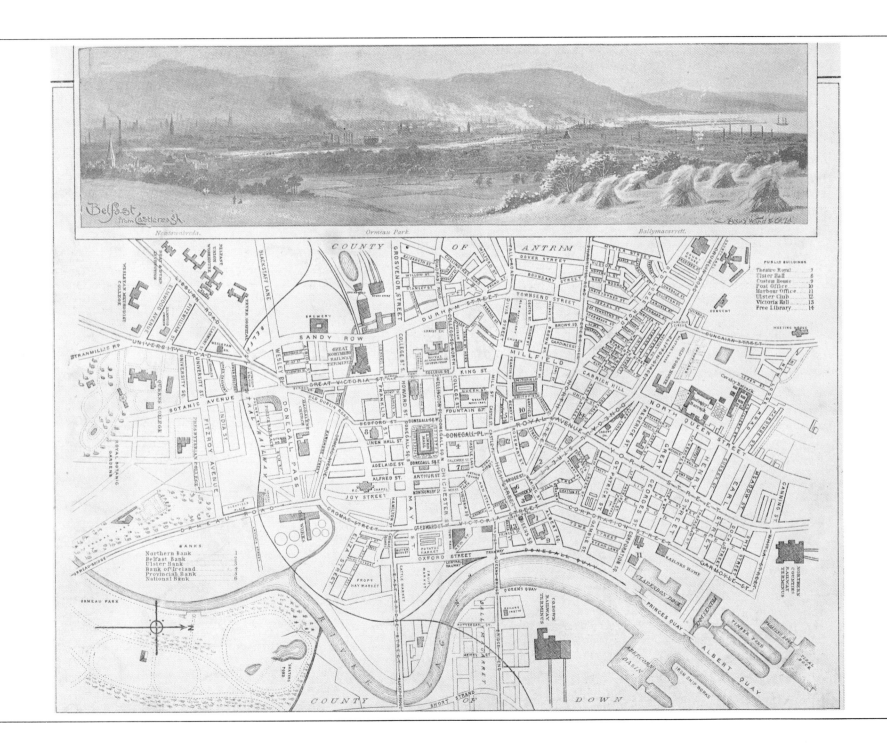

Belfast from Castlereagh

Newtownbreda.    Ormeau Park.    Ballymacarrett.

PUBLIC BUILDINGS.

Theatre Royal ....... 7
Ulster Hall ......... 8
Custom House ....... 9
Post Office ......... 10
Harbour Office ..... 11
Ulster Club ........ 12
Victoria Hall ...... 13
Free Library ....... 14

BANKS.

Northern Bank ........ 1
Belfast Bank ......... 2
Ulster Bank .......... 3
Bank of Ireland ...... 4
Provincial Bank ...... 5
National Bank ........ 6

# INTRODUCTION

THE FIFTH day of November 1888 was a special occasion for the people of Belfast. On that date Belfast ceased to be a town and was officially designated a city. Since the population of the new city numbered nearly a quarter of a million inhabitants this event can have come as no surprise to contemporaries but it did serve to highlight the remarkable transformation which was taking place in Belfast. At the beginning of the century, the town had been inhabited by under 20,000 people and even in 1851 there were only 97,784 residents. In the second half of the nineteenth century, however, Belfast experienced a rate of growth unequalled by any other urban centre in the British Isles.[1] By 1901 the citizens numbered 349,180; a decade later the figure stood at 386, 947.

Most of the photographs in this book were taken between 1880 and 1914, although a few date from the early 1870s. They present a striking picture of the new, bustling city which emerged in the late Victorian and Edwardian eras. They show how the old Georgian town was transformed with the development of main thoroughfares, the provision of parks and the erection of many fine new buildings, including not only shops, warehouses, factories and mills, but also theatres, churches, hospitals and schools. The port, with its numerous ships and its thriving docks and quays, is vividly recorded. Linen manufacture and shipbuilding, the two main sources of Belfast's growth and prosperity, are also dramatically illustrated.

This impressive new city did, of course, have its darker side. As in other industrial centres of the time, conditions of employment were often harsh, and housing in certain areas was very inadequate. There were sporadic outbreaks of sectarian animosity. Nonetheless, the Belfast which grew up was a remarkable achievement, based on few natural resources but on the efforts of 'an energetic and enterprising people'.[2] It provided a vibrant new community for the large numbers of inhabitants who had flocked in from the countryside: it has been estimated that in 1901 only one fifth of the householders living in the city had actually been born there.[3] Above all, in its busy workplaces it provided employment in a land where emigration was commonplace.

Map and view of Belfast, 1897, from
*Views of Belfast and the County Down*
(Dublin, 1897).

# The photographs and the photographer

All these photographs come from the Lawrence Collection in the National Library of Ireland. They belonged originally to the photographic business of William Mervin Lawrence of Dublin. Thanks to the research of Kieran Hickey, however, we know that they were mostly the work of Lawrence's outstanding chief photographer, Robert French (1841-1917)[4]. Between 1880 and 1914 French travelled regularly around Ireland, taking thousands of photographs to be used for lantern slides, postcards, guidebooks and advertisements. His photographs are for us today an extremely important record of life in Ireland at the turn of the century. But it must be remembered that French was only interested in scenes which were suitable for his employer's business. Thus, while his work illustrates well the main streets and the principal buildings of Belfast, there are no views of the city's many small streets of working-class houses; and linen manufacture and shipbuilding are the only two industries which are covered.

Difficulties arise in relation to dating the photographs. The original plates are not marked according to date and no records have survived as to when the photographs were taken. In this book an attempt has been made to date as many photographs as possible by using evidence from the actual views. The presence of trams or tramlines is often a useful guide. Horsedrawn trams were first introduced to Belfast in 1872 and continued in service until 1905 when electric trams were introduced. When horsedrawn trams are present and no other evidence is available the photographs have been dated c.1895: where electric trams are shown and there is no other information, the photographs are dated c.1906. Some views appeared in the 1897 Lawrence publication *Views of Belfast and the County Down* (Dublin) and they have also been dated c.1895. When dating is achieved from different evidence, such as the names of shopkeepers or of ships, this is normally made clear in the text. If no comment is made on the date, it can be assumed only that the photograph was taken between 1880 and 1914.

# The buildings and the architects

In the text accompanying the photographs, special attention has been paid to the architects who were responsible for designing this new and vital city. By Robert French's time, restrained Georgian classicism was long out of favour, displaced by successive revival fashions. A couple of Georgian buildings could not be omitted from his photographs, however, as much for their historical importance as for their impending demolition. St Anne's Church and the White Linen Hall reflect the enlightened example and encouragement of the fifth earl of Donegall whose programme of granting long leases and setting building standards resulted in the town's regular late-Georgian character. The two buildings also give a glimpse of the current state of architectural design; the more sophisticated church was designed by an accomplished Warwickshire architect, Francis Hiorne, while the less integrated Linen Hall was the work of Roger Mulholland, a local carpenter who had some success in property development. Later than either and much more severely Neo-classical is St George's Church in High Street by the Dubliner John Bowden. Although some local men were capable of such correct classicism, their work barely appears in the photographs; only Thomas Jackson is represented and even then by later buildings.

When Queen Victoria came to the throne, Charles Lanyon, a young engineer from Sussex, had been County Surveyor of Antrim for a year. Energetic, industrious, efficient, and endowed with ample charm, Lanyon more than anyone established the status and authority of the architect in Ulster as a professional man, rather than simply a builder who could draw a bit. His buildings had a metropolitan assurance; typically early Victorian, each was built in an historical style which could be associated with the modern use. Churches became gothic to be more honestly Christian like their medieval predecessors; banks looked like Florentine palaces, the homes of great renaissance bankers; colleges and schools became Tudor to be associated with the learning of ancient universities.

Under the influence of John Ruskin the succeeding generation mixed historical styles and contrasting colours in an entirely original way. In the work of Lanyon's partner, William Henry Lynn, and their rival from Newry, William James Barre, is the earliest echo of the 'Ruskinian Gothic' style invented by Deane and Woodward in Cork and Dublin. The popularity of the style during the 1860s and 1870s may be seen in the photographs in the work of Timothy Hevey, John Lanyon, William Batt, William Fogerty and Anthony Jackson, and it is a sign of the strength of the local profession that of these only Fogerty came from outside Belfast.

Towards the end of the century when French was taking his photographs, architects returned to the revival of a single style for each building. Classical and gothic are no longer mixed, and buildings got much larger. This development may be seen in the depicted buildings by W. J. Fennell, James Owen, John O'Shea and E. J. Byrne, and similarly in the ecclesiastical work of Sir Thomas Drew, J. J. McDonnell, and Samuel Close. Grandest of all were the great series of stores and offices designed by Robert Young, and his assistant and later partner, John Mackenzie. Young's son and grandson continued the business, and today 'Young and Mackenzie' is the only Belfast architectural practice to survive from Victorian times.

Less well represented in the views but more architecturally adventurous was the arts-and-crafts and *art-nouveau* work of the younger architects working around 1900, especially Vincent Craig, Alfred Forman and Frederick Tulloch. This period, too, saw the intervention of specialist architects from England with designs for the Royal Victoria Hospital, the Reform Club, and several theatres. More surprising was the inability of local architects to compete successfully against a youthful Londoner, Alfred Brumwell Thomas, in designing the City Hall. Perhaps only an Englishman could have adapted so many pieces of Wren's St Paul's Cathedral to create such a novel design. Certainly there can be few such signal demonstrations of how Belfast had advanced in self-confidence and prosperity than to compare this masterpiece of the Baroque revival with the Old Town Hall built less than thirty years before.

Through the medium of Robert French's remarkable photography we may still see this great transformation taking place. His work reveals the fine thoroughfares, buildings and institutions which so clearly reflect the enterprise, industry and aspirations of the citizens who created them. That age of confidence and prosperity left a rich legacy to Belfast, a legacy which has not always been used wisely. About a third of the major buildings shown in the photographs have gone; more have been radically altered. Yet despite widespread destruction and inappropriate development much of quality remains from French's time. The present generation would do well, while the opportunity lasts, to cherish and conserve what is best of the past, and to ensure that new fabric is worthy of its situation. In this way the future Belfast may still deserve acknowledgement as 'no mean city'.

## Arrangement of photographs

The plates in the book have been organised in the manner of a typical turn-of-the-century guide book to Belfast. We begin with a tour of the streets. Castle Place, at the heart of the city and at the centre of the tramway system, is a natural starting point. We proceed first to High Street and Victoria Street before returning to Castle Place. Then we go southwards through Donegall Place and Square, to Great Victoria Street, the Queen's University area and beyond. Starting once again from Castle Place (page 60) the tour proceeds northwards along Royal Avenue to York Street, Carlisle Circus and even to Cave Hill. Then comes a visit to the port and harbour. Finally there is a look at linen manufacture and ship building.

An Edwardian wearing a good pair of boots could have seen most of these sights during a Sunday walk. Modern faster man could probably do the same in a couple of hours but too often roars past unseeing. We hope you enjoy the tour.

# STREETS
## OF THE
# CITY

## CASTLE PLACE

Castle Place takes its name from the great house built by Sir Arthur Chichester, around which the town developed in the seventeenth century. The Castle stood just to the south of the present open space in Castle Place beneath which runs in culverts the River Farset.

The original Bank Buildings, standing on the bank of the river, was a fine Georgian building which faced east towards High Street. This view shows the second Bank Buildings, designed in the spirit of a palazzo of a renaissance Florentine banker. It was built for modern commercial purposes for the drapers Hawkins, Ledlie and Ferguson just before the middle of the nineteenth century.[1] Next door can be seen the Provincial Bank, then set back from the narrow Hercules Place (see p. 60).

The dominant building on the north side of the open space was the Ulster Club of 1861, a rather hefty slice of Brighton with its bow front, designed by Charles Lanyon;[2] the demolition of this building in 1981 has left a sad gap in Castle Place. Absence of tramlines in the photograph reveals it was taken before August 1872.

## CASTLE PLACE (right)

Castle Place was the centre of the tramway system, or Castle Junction as it was called. In this view, c.1906, the third Bank Buildings, proprietors Robertson, Ledlie and Ferguson, now presides over the junction, and is about twice the height of the previous building. Completed in 1900 under the direction of W. H. Lynn, who was then over 70, it is a monument to this architect's continued innovative powers.[1]

Though outwardly just a good example of late-Victorian, overblown classicism, the building is in reality not stone-built but depends on Belfast's first large skeletal steel frame. Thus, though representative of the city's great period of architectural growth, the Bank Buildings anticipates the age of the sky-scraper.

To the left, at the corner of Donegall Place and Castle Street is Anderson and McAuley's new building, erected in 1890 (see pp 14-15). On the right, turning the curve into Lombard Street, are Robb's grand new premises, built in the 1870s. Castle Place was the centre of the tramway system, or Castle Junction as it was called.

CASTLE PLACE BELFAST. 318. W.L.

## CORNMARKET

On the left of this view is the tea warehouse of Forster Green and Co. An advertisement of 1913 sang the praises of its tea: 'From the land of Golden Fleece to the Orkneys it is known and called for by all sorts of people, commoner and king, autocrat and democrat'.[1] These premises were built in 1868 to designs by Thomas Jackson and they occupied the site of the seventeenth-century market-house.[2]

The tall polychrome building in the distance, at the junction of Arthur Square and Anne Street, is the Masonic Hall.[3] Despite the contrast with Forster Green's, it also dates from 1868 and was designed by Lanyon, Lynn and Lanyon. The handle bars on the bicycle in the foreground are an 1890's style, so it is possible that the photograph was taken during this decade.

## THEATRE ROYAL, ARTHUR SQUARE

The original theatre on this site opened in 1793.[1] Its successor, designed by Charles Sherry, was opened in 1871 and was badly damaged by fire ten years later.[2] This photograph shows the third Theatre Royal which was rebuilt by C. J. Phipps. Sherry's façade is still largely intact but it lacks its original, giant surmounting pediment with its bold royal arms. There are Shakespearean character busts on the façade.

The commercial success of the new theatre enabled the owner, J. F. Warden, to launch the Grand Opera House in 1895.[3] Until the 1870's entertainment at the Theatre Royal was provided mainly by local artistes but from this time, thanks partly to improved transport facilities, travelling companies such as the D'Oyly Carte and Carla Rosa became the mainstay of the house, apart from two periods, 1895-1904 and 1909-15, when it ran as a variety theatre.

By 1910 Belfast was served not only by the Theatre Royal, but also by the Grand Opera House, the Empire, the Royal Hippodrome and the Alhambra. The Theatre Royal was restructured in 1915 as the Royal cinema and was demolished in 1961.[4]

## HIGH STREET

These two photographs of High Street show the rapidly changing character of central Belfast in the late nineteenth and early twentieth centuries. In the earlier view on the left, dated before August 1872, many Georgian houses survive, often with new shop fronts; tram lines have not yet been laid. In the later one, taller four-storey buildings predominate.

The West of England Cloth Merchants' building is in both views, but note how the neighbouring buildings change. The view on the right can be dated about 1910 by the presence of the electric trams and a motor car. It is interesting to observe the four-wheeled open carriage (or landau) with its mounted escort which is approaching in the middle of the road in this second photograph. Clearly the vehicle was carrying someone important—perhaps with all the flags on display it was a visit of the lord lieutenant.

High Street is actually Belfast's earliest main thoroughfare and it follows the irregular line of the Farset river which still flows underneath its centre. Many of the buildings on the left were destroyed during the blitz in the Second World War.[1]

HIGH ST. BELFAST. 2415. W.L.

ST.GEORGE'S CHURCH.BELFAST.2678.W.L.

## ST GEORGE'S CHURCH OF IRELAND CHURCH, HIGH STREET

Built in 1816 on the site of the seventeenth-century corporation church, St George's was designed by John Bowden of Dublin.[1] It incorporates the portico of Ballyscullion House near Lough Beg, Co. Londonderry. This house had been begun by Frederick Hervey, Bishop of Derry and Earl of Bristol, but remained unfinished when the Earl-Bishop died in 1803.[2] Ten years later the portico was purchased for St George's, which was built as a chapel of ease for St Anne's (see p. 69).

As may be seen from this angled view the rest of the church was rather plain. Even so, St George's marks the beginning of a fashion for serious neo-classical building in Belfast. Churches and public buildings, as well as many private houses, appeared with pediments and cornices or a portico on a couple of columns.

The church today looks much the same as when this photograph was taken, although it now lacks neighbours on either side. The railing and gatepiers are being restored.

## THE NATIONAL BANK, HIGH STREET

This view of 1900 gives a clear demonstration of how the buildings of High Street developed. Mortimer's on the right was probably built in the eighteenth century. The board attached to the dormer window in its steeply-pitched roof was to stop an accumulation of snow suddenly falling onto people on the pavement as there was not even a gutter to prevent this.

On the left there are more decorative Victorian premises; the vacant shop enables us to date the photograph. Last and largest in the sequence is the National Bank. By contrast its scale is enormous; the first floor alone reaches to the roofs of its neighbours. Its sculpture is elaborate and intentionally impressive—the sort of place you could trust with your savings. The date on the gable refers to when the Bank was first established. The architect of the Belfast branch was William Batt.

Built in 1894-97, it had all the latest banking equipment including a burglar-proof safe, which was wired to the manager's bedroom.[1] Of these buildings only the bank now survives, dwarfed by River House, built in the late 1960s. In 1966 the National Bank was taken over by the Bank of Ireland.

## THE ALBERT MEMORIAL CLOCK, QUEEN'S SQUARE

This imposing clock tower, 145 feet high, was completed in mid 1869. It is a free adaptation of an Italian campanile and was designed by W. J. Barre who died before the work was finished.[1] Like the best campaniles, it leans a bit.

It was erected in memory of the Prince Consort, whose full-length statue by S. F. Lynn stands upon an ornamented pedestal in a niche in front of the tower.[2] This view is dated c.1895. Beyond the tower in Queen's Square there may be seen to the left, the head office of the Northern Bank (built 1851)[3] and the Custom House (built 1857).

A meeting or rally is taking place behind the clock in the square; the steps of the Custom House beyond became Belfast's equivalent of the Speakers' Corner.

## ULSTER BANK HEAD-OFFICE, WARING STREET

Established in 1836 the Ulster Banking Company expanded with the commercial growth of Belfast and by the 1850s required a prestigious headquarters. Following a competition, this new head-office was erected to designs 'of Roman character' by the Glaswegian, James Hamilton[1]

Completed in 1860, the building created something of a stir in Belfast: the town was not used to quite such a show of sculptural and decorative details. The carved figures on the honey-coloured sandstone building, representing Britannia supported by Justice and Commerce, were the work of Thomas Fitzpatrick who was responsible for the carving on the Custom House.[2]

Hamilton, the architect, moved to Belfast and designed other Ulster banks for Sligo and Trim as well as Ewart's fine warehouse in Bedford Street. Today the tall urns on top of the bank in Waring Street have gone but the gates and lamps have survived.

## VICTORIA STREET

This fine, wide thoroughfare was opened by the town commissioners in the late 1840s and called Victoria after the royal visit of 1849. Following the building of Donegall Quay the street was cut through from the markets to the foot of High Street along the line of two parallel alleys, Weigh House Lane and Forrest Lane.[1]

The opening on the left leads into Victoria Square, originally Poultry Square which stood at the head of a dock reaching in from the river. The cast-iron fountain and canopy at the square was a memorial of 1874 to Daniel Joseph Jaffé (now moved to the King's Bridge).[1] Jaffé, a linen merchant originally from Hamburg, built Belfast's first synagogue, and was father of Sir Otto Jaffé, Lord Mayor 1899-1900 and 1904-5.

Various imposing commercial buildings were constructed along the new Victoria Street and in the late 1860s it was chosen as a suitably prominent site for the new town hall, seen here on the right of this photograph, taken *c.*1906.

## THE TOWN HALL, VICTORIA STREET

Built according to designs by Anthony Jackson of Belfast, which were chosen in a competition held in 1869, the Town Hall was officially opened in 1870, and remained Belfast's principal administrative building until the completion of the City Hall in 1906.[1]

The Venetian gothic style, which mixes historic elements from different countries, derives both from the writings of John Ruskin and from the architectural example of Deane and Woodward. But Jackson also used drawings he himself made on holiday in Italy in 1864, many of which are now in the Ulster Museum.[2] Though most of the features derive from Italy (boldly arched windows, colonnettes set into the corners, and porches supported on corbel-brackett columns), some, such as the tall French mansard roof, are not.

It was a sign of changing public attitude towards ostentatious building (see p.11, Ulster Bank) that this building was criticised for not being sufficiently impressive and a parapet was added following public agitation. This early view, probably of the 1880s, shows the town hall before the addition of the entrance canopy with its fish-scale roof.

## DONEGALL PLACE

Only some thirty years separate these two views of Donegall Place, as seen from Castle Junction, but in that time enormous changes have occurred. The street on the right, photographed *c*.1908, has as its focus the newly-built city hall with a much larger silhouette than its predecessor, the White Linen hall, seen on the left in a picture of the early 1880s.[1]

Between those times the Bank Buildings, to the extreme right, has been rebuilt (see p. 3), while beyond it across Castle Street Anderson and Macauley's store has been greatly enlarged and reconstructed to designs by Young and Mackenzie in 1890.[2] It was intended to have a turret with a conical roof above the clock at Anderson and Macauley's although this did not materialise; instead there is a large bell in an open frame. Beyond this is Donegall Place Buildings, constructed as shops and offices, *c*.1868.

Note how the buildings along the street in the photographs show the gradual change from small houses of Georgian scale, only three windows wide and three storeys high, to taller, wider, more elaborate offices and department stores. By 1892 Donegall Place was being described as the Bond Street of Belfast: 'It is distinguished by some of the most select and fashionable shops and mercantile emporia in the city.'[3]

## IMPERIAL HOTEL, DONEGALL PLACE

Situated on the east side of Donegall Place at the Castle Lane junction, the Imperial was Belfast's best known hotel at the turn of the century.

A fine late-Georgian building, it had been enlarged with two new storeys, one with a French mansard roof, to the designs of Sherry and Hughes in 1868.[1] There were 120 beds in the hotel and, according to an account of 1892, it contained baths (something new to the late-Victorian traveller), commercial, coffee, billiard, and dining rooms, and had extensive stabling accommodation nearby.

The proprietor, W. J. Jury, was a well known personality and the blender of special liquors such as 'Special Jury Whiskey'.[2] Next door to the Imperial is Reuben Payne's Bazaar with its fine neo-classical façade. A merchant tailor and clothier, Payne gave up the premises c.1895 so the photograph probably dates from the early 1890s.

## QUEEN'S ARCADE, DONEGALL PLACE

On the west side of Donegall Place, the arcade was built in 1880 to designs of James McKinnon, Belfast's town engineer: from the homes of the shopkeepers, it is clear that this photograph was taken shortly after it opened. The building provided covered access to thirty small shops. The glazed pavement cover, added to the Castle Restaurant façade in 1887 by James Phillips, sheltered generations of shoppers from the rain.[1]

Both arcade and restaurant were built for George Fisher who personally ran the latter with its various eating rooms. 'Dinners à la carte, luncheons, breakfasts and teas, suppers and contract parties are all supplied here, and in every case the perfection of viands and service is the great characteristic of the place'.[2]

## DONEGALL PLACE

Donegall Place was built as the principal, smart, residential thoroughfare in late eighteenth-century Belfast. Both these views were taken through the gates of the White Linen Hall and only some ten years separate them, but important developments have taken place in this time.

In the left hand picture, taken c.1870, this end of Donegall Place is still partly residential in character; trams have not yet appeared. There are two fine Georgian houses on the right, although beyond them is the Bank of Ireland, which was designed 1858-9 by Sandham Symes of Dublin, to look like a Florentine merchant's palazzo.[1] On the left is the Royal Hotel, formerly the town residence of the Donegall family,[2] landlords of Belfast: Charles Dickens and Thackeray are supposed to have stayed in this hotel.[3]

In the second picture, however, the two Georgian houses and their garden have been replaced by Robinson and Cleaver's. A shop and offices for the Singer Sewing Machine Company have been built in the garden of the Royal Hotel. We can tell this later view was taken c.1888, as there remains one last row of windows to be added to Robinson and Cleaver's in the gap next to the Bank of Ireland.

Notice how the vista in the early photograph is blocked by the end of Castle Place and the beginning of Hercules Street while in the 1888 photograph the view looks straight down the newly opened Royal Avenue (see pp 60-61).

## DONEGALL SQUARE NORTH

The premises on the left are the linen warehouse of Moore and Weinberg, which was built in 1864 by Lanyon, Lynn and Lanyon.[1] The front portico columns have gone but otherwise the building survives now as the home of the Linen Hall Library.

Following the acquisition of the White Linen Hall by the corporation as a site for the new city hall, the library moved to this side of Donegall Square in 1896. This view, taken c. 1886, shows gardens in front of the houses beside the Moore and Weinberg building and also at the end of Donegall Place.

POSTAL TELEGRAPH OFFICE.

RICHARDSON SONS AND
OWDEN'S LINEN WAREHOUSE
DONEGALL SQUARE NORTH

This building, on the north-east side of Donegall Square, was constructed in 1886-9 to the design of Lanyon, Lynn and Lanyon. It was perhaps the greatest achievement in the Ruskinian gothic style of the firm which led the way in this style in Belfast.

It served as the headquarters and warehouse for the firm of Richardson Son and Owden.[1] Well laid out showrooms contained displays of white linens, damasks, embroidery and handkerchiefs. Busy packing rooms despatched goods all over the world. When built it was the largest linen warehouse in Belfast. During air raids in the Second World War the mansard roof was destroyed.

It is now owned by Marks and Spencer who are replacing the roof and converting the interior into shopping space. This photograph was taken in the 1880s: Robinson and Cleaver's store has not yet been built.

## ROBINSON AND CLEAVER, DONEGALL SQUARE NORTH

Edward Robinson and John Cleaver commenced business in Castle Place in 1870 and they were so successful that they commissioned the firm of Young and Mackenzie to design their new Royal Irish Linen Warehouse at the corner of Donegall Place and Donegall Square North.

Built in an overblown Italianate style which these architects made very popular in late Victorian Belfast, this colossal department store opened in 1888.[1] It contained many wonders such as electric light, supplied with power from engines in the basement, and a 'luxurious passenger elevator of the latest and best American type'.[2] The front of the building was enriched by elaborate carving, which included busts of the firm's most distinguished customers such as Queen Victoria, the Crown Prince of Germany, and, not forgetting, the Maharajah of Cooch Behar.[3]

The grounds of the White Linen Hall have not yet been cordoned off for the building of the new city hall so this photograph on the left is dated c.1890.

The view on the right shows the fine central staircase of the store. The firm had a special interest in products of Irish manufacture, especially linen, and built up an important overseas postal business.

## THE WHITE LINEN HALL, DONEGALL SQUARE

Occupying the centre of Donegall Square, the White Linen Hall was a two-storeyed quadrangular building. It was completed in 1785 and it is very probable that the architect was Roger Mulholland of Belfast.[1] Its original purpose was to serve as a linen market and exchange but with changes in the trade it ceased to be used for this.

From 1802 the premises housed the Belfast Library and Society for Promoting Knowledge which consequently became known as the Linen Hall Library. Other parts of the building were used as offices by linen firms. An 1884 guide to Belfast commented on the pleasing appearance of the premises and surroundings: "the grounds around the buildings are tastefully kept, and are open to the public. The foliage of the trees and shrubs imparts quite a rural appearance to this portion of the town.[2]"

The White Linen Hall was demolished by the corporation in the early 1890s to make way for the new city hall. These two photographs, taken in the late 1870s, show on the left an oblique view from Wellington Place and on the right a view inside the quadrangle.

CITY HALL. BELFAST. 2386, W.L.

## THE CITY HALL, DONEGALL SQUARE

It was indicative of the growth of prosperity and consequent self-confidence in late-Victorian Belfast that by the late 1880s it was felt that the town hall in Victoria Street was inadequate as municipal headquarters.

The White Linen Hall was purchased as a site in 1890 and six years later a public architectural competition was held for the new building. The winner was Brumwell Thomas, a London Architect.[1] The work began in 1898 and the city hall was declared open in August 1906. The photograph on the left must have been taken shortly after this event. While the exterior is imposing, the interior is an even more lavish Wrenaissance style which was then popular; many of the details are copied from St Paul's Cathedral, London.

The view on the right shows the council chamber with its seating arranged on the model of the house of commons with a central gangway. According to tradition, profits from the gas works made such a building possible. In any case, the end result is one of the most significant municipal centres in the British Isles.[2]

## DONEGALL SQUARE EAST

The Ocean Accident Insurance Buildings, built to designs by Young and Mackenzie, 1900-2, broke very confidently with the scale and style of late-Georgian Belfast.[1] The four-storey brick houses to each side, with classical doorways and regular façades, were built early in the nineteenth century. The first two houses on the left in Chichester Street are the offices of L'Estrange and Brett, solicitors.[2] The Linenhall Hotel was demolished in the 1920s to make way for Imperial House, a block of offices. Barely in sight on the right is Donegall Square Methodist Church, completed in 1850 to designs by Isaac Farrell,[3] and the last prominent Belfast church to be built in a full-blooded classical revival style (see p. 76).

## SCOTTISH PROVIDENT INSTITUTION, DONEGALL SQUARE WEST

This grand classical block of offices and shops was built in parts between 1899 and 1902 to designs by Young and Mackenzie.[1] The extreme decorative and sculptural front is shown to great advantage with morning light raking across the façade.

The block replaced a terrace of late-Georgian houses which gradually changed during the Victorian period to use as offices (including that of Charles Lanyon). Over the tree on the left can be glimpsed the pyramidal roof of the Northern Bank of 1903, also designed by Young and Mackenzie. It was demolished with its neighbours in 1970 to make way for the new head office of the bank. The trees grew along the front of the old White Linen Hall which occupied the square.

The advertising hoarding was put up while the Linen Hall was demolished to make way for the new city hall and so this photograph must have been taken in the early 1900s. On the right is Wellington Place with the battlemented tower of the 'modified gothic' Y.M.C.A. Building, opened in 1895, and yet again the work of Young and Mackenzie.[2]

SCOTTISH PROVIDENT INSTITUTION. BELFAST. 2368.W.L.

## WELLINGTON PLACE

Incorrectly labelled as Linen Hall Street on the plate, this photograph is a rare, mid-1880s view of Wellington Place.

It shows on the right the Evangelical Union church, built in 1858 by John Boyd and demolished in 1895.[1] Beyond the church is the linen warehouse of James and Robert Young, designed by John Lanyon in 1877.[2] In the distance in College Square is the grand neo-classical façade of the Royal Belfast Academical Institution, designed to plans by Sir John Soane.[3] The main part of the building was completed in 1814.

Wellington Place, or South Parade as it was called originally, had been developed as a street of superior terrace residences in the 1790s but by the 1880s most of the buildings were used for commercial purposes.[4]

## COLLEGE SQUARE EAST

This mid-1880s photograph shows the fine early nineteenth-century houses which adorned the east side of College Square. As late as the 1890s this was still a prime residential area. Six out of ten residences in this terrace in 1890 were occupied by surgeons. Belfast's original medical school had been at Inst and this area continued to be the centre of Belfast's medical life.

By the end of the century, however, several buildings in this terrace had been converted for commerce and the rest soon followed. The statue is of Dr. Henry Cooke—popularly known as the Black Man. In 1876 this statue replaced one on the same plinth of the Earl of Belfast (1827-53).[1]

## FISHERWICK PLACE, GREAT VICTORIA STREET

This left hand view, *c.*1886, of Fisherwick Place running down to College Square East portrays well the quiet, residential nature of the area before the great changes which occurred at the turn of the century.

On the immediate right of the photograph one can see the railings and trees which stood in front of Fisherwick Place Presbyterian Church, at the junction with Howard Street. Designed like a Greek temple in 1828 by Thomas Duff,[1] it was considered unfashionable, even pagan, in the 1890s, by its congregation, many of whom had moved away from the city centre. So a new church was built (see p. 50)

and this one was demolished to make way for the new headquarters of the Presbyterian Church in Ireland.

The photograph to the right, taken *c.*1906 from 100 yards farther up Great Victoria Street, shows the new Fisherwick Place and College Square East. We can see the Church House and Assembly Hall at the corner of Howard Street. These were built in 1905; the architects were Young and Mackenzie.[2] The crown spire was considered suitably Scottish. At the far end of College Square East on the left hand side there is still scaffolding on the new municipal technical institute, which was opened in 1907.

THE
PALACE
TWICE 7 & 9 NIGHTLY

GREAT VICTORIA St. BELFAST. 3859. W.L.

## THE GRAND OPERA HOUSE, AND ROYAL HIPPODROME, GREAT VICTORIA STREET

On 16 December 1895 the Grand Opera House was formally opened by Frank Benson. It was the work of the leading theatre architect of the day, Frank Matcham of London. Describing the building as a 'perfect Eastern palace' the press loudly acclaimed the grand oriental style of the theatre, especially the interior.

Apart from a brief period, 1904 to 1909, when it became the Palace of Varieties, the opera house presented a mixed programme of entertainment, from touring drama and opera companies to the annual pantomime.[1] In 1961 it became a cinema but by 1976 its future was in jeopardy. In that latter year, however, it was acquired by the Arts Council of Northern Ireland which then restored the building under the direction of Mr Robert McKinstry. A superb example of a late Victorian theatre, it continues to excite the public. This photograph on the left was taken c.1900 before the building of the Hippodrome.

The Royal Hippodrome was designed by another theatre specialist, Bertie Crewe, a former assistant to Frank Matcham. It opened in 1907 as a popular variety theatre, offering twice-nightly performances. In 1931 the Hippodrome was converted into a cinema.[2] It still stands, although the exterior is hidden by modern cladding.

## KENSINGTON HOTEL, COLLEGE SQUARE EAST

Opened c.1911, the hotel was described in the 1914 Belfast directory as 'first-class family and commercial—strictly temperance.'[1] It received a lot of trade from people arriving at the nearby G.N.R. station. What is the man on the roof doing?

The hotel survived, under different ownership, until 1974 when it was closed due to bomb damage. The building was demolished in 1978.

## THE G.N.R. STATION, GREAT VICTORIA STREET

The first railway line in Ulster opened on 12 August 1839. It ran only 7½ miles from Belfast to Lisburn but by 1842 the line extended to Portadown and by 1849 it reached Armagh.[1] This was soon extended and the commercial success which ensued allowed the company, Ulster Railway, to build an imposing Belfast terminus and main office at Glengall Place (later part of Great Victoria Street).

The building was completed in 1846 under the direction of John Godwin, the company engineer who soon after became the first professor of civil engineering at the Queen's College, Belfast.[1] The canopy over the approach drive was added later. In 1876 the Great Northern Railway Company was formed from the original Ulster Railway and several southern companies, so linking the whole Belfast to Dublin line under one management.

The main portion of the building was demolished in 1967 to make way for the Europa (now Forum) Hotel. The left-hand pavilion and wing survived until 1974. Now only the engine shed with fine cast-iron survives as part of a bus station. The date of the photograph is c.1906, the time is 9.35 a.m. and the morning rush is over.

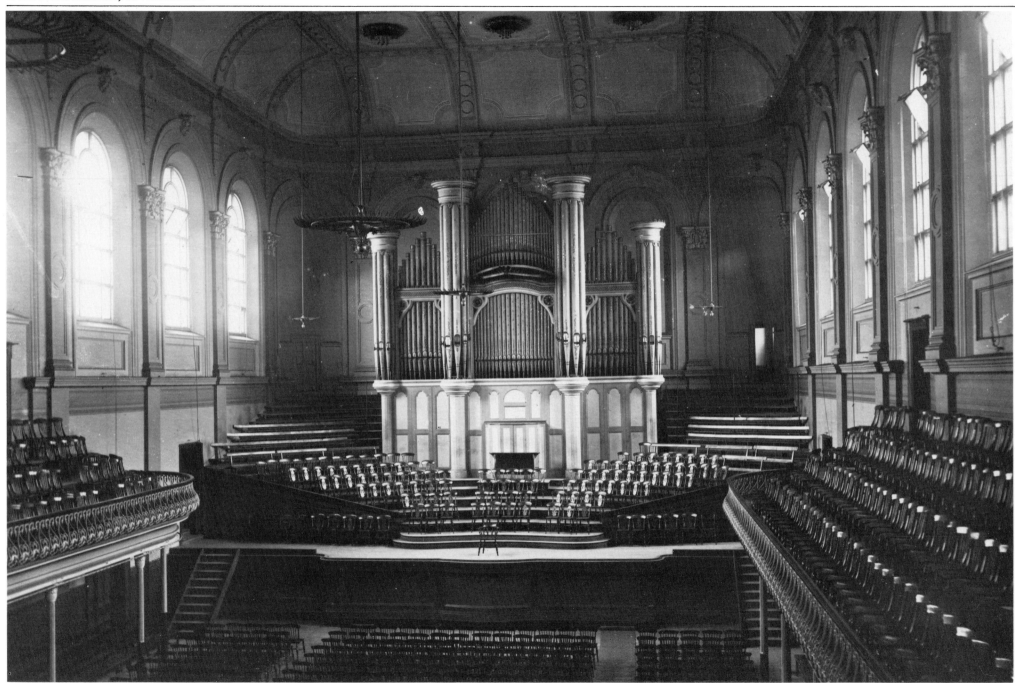

## ULSTER HALL, INTERIOR

The competition to design the Ulster Hall was won by a young Newry architect, W. J. Barre, who quickly moved to Belfast to supervise the building and to guard his interests against more established and jealous members of the profession in the town.[1]

By mid-Victorian standards the building was plain and dignified rather than showy. For the exterior Barre used the simple Italianate formula of a strongly channelled or rusticated ground-floor with all the decorations, columns and other classical features saved for the principal floor above. The view on the lower right shows the linen warehouse (now Bryson House) at the side of the Ulster Hall, a building designed also by Barre but in his more developed Venetian gothic style.

The photograph of the interior on the right shows the great organ presented by Andrew Mulholland in 1862, and restored under the patronage of his descendant, Lord Dunleath, in 1982.

## ULSTER HALL, BEDFORD STREET

The top view shows the entrance elevation as originally designed with an arcaded *porte-cochère* which allowed visitors to climb down from their coaches under cover. The bottom photograph illustrates the change made to the front of the hall after the addition of the glazed canopy when the original *porte-cochère* had been enclosed as an extension to the vestibule. The Ulster Hall was erected in 1862 as a concert room and a hall for public meetings. It was owned by a company until 1902 when it was taken over by the corporation.[1]

SHAFTESBURY SQUARE

From the shopkeepers' names we can tell, with the help of street directories, that this photograph on the left (of the south of the square) was taken in the late 1880s. The block of shops in the centre (demolished late 1960s) was built 1884-7 and called after the seventh earl of Shaftesbury.[1] By 1890 the rest of the square, formerly part of the Dublin Road, was also known by this name.

The premises on the right, built in 1868, are a good example of mid-Victorian Ruskinian polychrome building in white brick with red and blue brick decorations. The left part of this block still exists. McCusker's spirit grocers can be seen at the end of Donegall Pass while beyond lies the lower end of the still-residential Botanic Avenue,

constructed in the 1860s and 1870s.[2] The fine drinking fountain in the middle of the square was removed in 1932.[3]

Between Great Victoria Street and Dublin Road in this view on the right (of the north of the square), c.1906, stands the Magdalene school-house, designed in the office of Charles Lanyon and opened in 1853.[4] The building later became a Sunday school and parochial hall, but was demolished in 1930 and replaced by shops and eventually a branch of the Ulster Bank. Most of the houses on the left side of the square were residential until the late 1890s when shops were installed at ground level.

## PRESBYTERIAN COLLEGE, COLLEGE PARK

Erected in 1853 for the training of students for the presbyterian ministry, this building is one of the finest architectural set-pieces designed in the office of Charles Lanyon.[1]

Built close to the recently-completed Queen's College, it may have been intended as something of an architectural rebuke. At this time presbyterians eschewed the use of rivived gothic style, even in its latest Tudor-collegiate form as at Queen's, because of its association with Pugin (see p. 77). Lanyon also, of course, architect of Queen's, provided instead a dignified classical building.

Nevertheless the details, especially to students of classical archaeology, are irreverently mannerist. For example, the great attached Tuscan columns of the portico carry nothing more significant than their own entablatures and the flippant scrolls and urns of the attic. The college was later known as Assembly's College and is now called Union Theological College. The main difference in this view today is the presence of the mature trees which add so much to the character of the Queen's area.

## DEAF AND DUMB INSTITUTE, LISBURN ROAD

This well-designed and expensively-executed institutional building stood on the site now occupied by Queen's Medical Biology Centre, facing across Lisburn Road to Elmwood Avenue. It was built in 1845 to plans by Charles Lanyon, and has been seen as a forerunner to the same architect's Queen's College, which was designed a year or two later.[1]

In many ways, however, it was a more original scheme, and such details as the combination of shaped gables of Jacobean type with Tudor crown finials suggest a less slavish attitude towards adherence to a single past style. In this the building anticipates the mixing of styles of High Victorian buildings (see pp 21 and 60).

The society which ran the institute was one of a number of such philanthropic charities which emerged in Belfast before official public health care.[2] The building was demolished in 1965.

## HAMILTON TOWER, QUEEN'S COLLEGE

In 1878 Queen's College, Belfast, became a constituent college of the Royal University of Ireland and thirty years later it was made a university in its own right. During this time various additions were made to the buildings at Queen's, especially in the last decade of the nineteenth century and the first decade of the twentieth.

This porter's gate lodge and tower was erected in 1906 in honour of the Rev. Thomas Hamilton, president of the college, 1889-1908, and later vice-chancellor of the university, 1908-23. It was designed by Dr Robert Cochrane, architect to the board of works in Dublin, as were the surviving south wing and tower of the college.[1]

In common with all the university buildings until the arrival of the Whitla Hall, Hamilton Tower was in the Tudor-revival style. The tower, however, had a short career and was removed in 1922. On the original plate Queen's is still called a college so it is likely that this photograph was taken between 1906 and 1908.

## QUEEN'S COLLEGE, UNIVERSITY ROAD

The Queen's Colleges, one of which was in Belfast, were founded by an act of parliament in 1845.[1] This was in response to the need for more higher educational facilities in Ireland and also to the objections of presbyterians and catholics that Trinity College, Dublin, was still dominated by members of the Church of Ireland.

Designs for the Belfast college were by Charles Lanyon. The buildings were inspected just prior to the college's opening by Queen Victoria and Prince Albert. At the time of the royal visit there was a very serious cholera epidemic in the town and the unoccupied college was the only building where the Queen visited the interior.[2]

Early Victorian architects, such as Lanyon, chose building styles for their historical associations. Queen's is a free translation of the Founder's Tower and other elements of Magdalen College at Oxford. The intention was to provide the new college with an architectural setting imbued with ancient learning and scholarly tradition.[3] So Belfast has a Tudor-revival university college, and many of the province's other colleges and schools were built in this style for the same reasons.

The main block at Queen's has changed little while the gardens and trees have now a rich maturity.

ENTRANCE GATE. QUEENS COLLEGE. BELFAST. 10096. W.L.

## METHODIST COLLEGE, COLLEGE GARDENS

The college is seen here from University Road looking south-west over the main college gateway on the left and the closed gates to the houses facing the college in College Gardens, just out of the view to the right.

The college was opened in 1868 to provide training for candidates to the methodist ministry as well as a general education for other pupils. It was designed by William Fogerty of Limerick.[1] Although the basic plan of central tower with wings follows the layout of Queen's College close by (see p. 44), this later building mixes historic styles, especially French and English gothic, in typically High Victorian manner.

This view is obviously earlier than the one opposite because of the horse-drawn tram, and can be dated *c*.1900. Other Belfast schools which were opened in this period include Victoria College (1859) and Campbell College (1894); St Malachy's was founded in 1833 but its main buildings were constructed in the 1870s.

BOTANIC GARDENS ENTRANCE, AT JUNCTION OF
UNIVERSITY, STRANMILLIS AND MALONE ROADS

The Botanic main gate lodge was designed in 1879 by William Batt.[1]
As seen here, *c.*1907, it was a fine little example of the Ruskinian or
Venetian gothic style, built of mixed brick and stone, with a corner
clock tower set over an arched portico with vigorous carvings.

The demolition of the lodge in 1965 was unnecessary in that the site
remains empty; it was also unfortunate in removing an important
architectural focus for this busy junction, and a feature which gave
arrival at the Botanic Gardens a sense of occasion.

Abbotsford House (built 1889[2]), between the Stranmillis and
Malone Roads, is a good example of the later Victorian delight in
using the irregularity of urban street patterns to architectural
advantage. The design moulds the alignment of both streets into a
unified composition with a tall roof and shaped gable providing a
focus for University Road. Note that the tram is one of the covered
version introduced from 1907.

## THE PALM HOUSE, BOTANIC GARDENS

The Botanic Gardens were established by a private society in 1827 and moved to the present site two years later.[1] One reason for the opening of Queen's College twenty years later in a place then rather remote from the town centre was the proximity of the gardens.

The wings of the Palm House, built 1839-40 by Richard Turner under the architectural supervision of Charles Lanyon, are one of the earliest surviving examples of the use of curvilinear glass and cast-iron.[2] This type of construction was pioneered by Turner at the Hammersmith Iron Foundry in Dublin from 1834. Two of his other works, both later than Belfast, are the houses at Glasnevin and the great Palm House at Kew. When the central dome was added to a modified design in 1852, Messrs Young of Glasgow did the ironwork.

After a full restoration, the Palm House and the adjacent Tropical Ravine House (1886) were reopened in 1983. This work was carried out by Belfast City Council to which the gardens were transferred in 1895 as a public promenade.

## BELFAST BOAT CLUB HOUSE, STRANMILLIS

This fine boat house was opened, on 28 May 1898, very appropriately by Mrs Margaret Pirrie, wife of W. J. Pirrie, head of Harland and Wolff. The building has been designed by a committee of the Belfast Boat Club, assisted by an architect member, Vincent Craig, a brother of the first Lord Craigavon.[1]

An opening ceremony arranged for the previous year had been postponed when it was discovered that two of the iron columns supporting the balcony had sunk about four inches. In spite of this hesitant beginning, however, this fine 'freestyle' building served the club well until its destruction by a bomb in 1972. Boats were stored on the ground floor while on the second storey there were changing rooms and a committee room.

The club house was actually situated on an island with the Lagan navigation at the front, as seen here in this photograph, and the River Lagan at the back. A small punt conveyed members across the canal until 1963 when it was filled in.

## FISHERWICK PRESBYTERIAN CHURCH, AT CHLORINE GARDENS, MALONE ROAD

The original church stood at Fisherwick Place, but it was demolished at the turn of the century and the site was used for the new Presbyterian Church House and Assembly Buildings.

The new church was built in 1902 on the Malone Road. It was designed by Samuel Close.[1] Most of this architect's churches were built for the Church of Ireland and Fisherwick's character is more episcopalian than many gothic presbyterian churches of its generation, with clearly defined aisles and transepts. The twin portals at the front, however, are a clear indication that this is a presbyterian church, relating as they normally do to twin aisles and a central pulpit facing a central block of pews. This was the case at Fisherwick until a decade ago when the church was refurbished with a middle aisle.

No. 50 Malone Road on the right was built in 1892[2] as a private home. Its hefty classical charms now provide shelter for part of the Queen's University architecture department.

## ST BRIGID'S CATHOLIC CHURCH, DERRYVOLGIE AVENUE

St Brigid's was built as a daughter church of St Malachy's in Alfred Street. The architect was J. J. McDonnell[1] and the foundation stone was laid on 10 July 1891. The polychrome brick construction and round-arched openings orginate, appropriately enough, in the Italian Romanesque architecture so admired by John Ruskin.

More Irish altogether are the wheel-cross gable finials. The original gabled porch has been replaced with a much wider vestibule which is in marked stylistic contrast to the church.

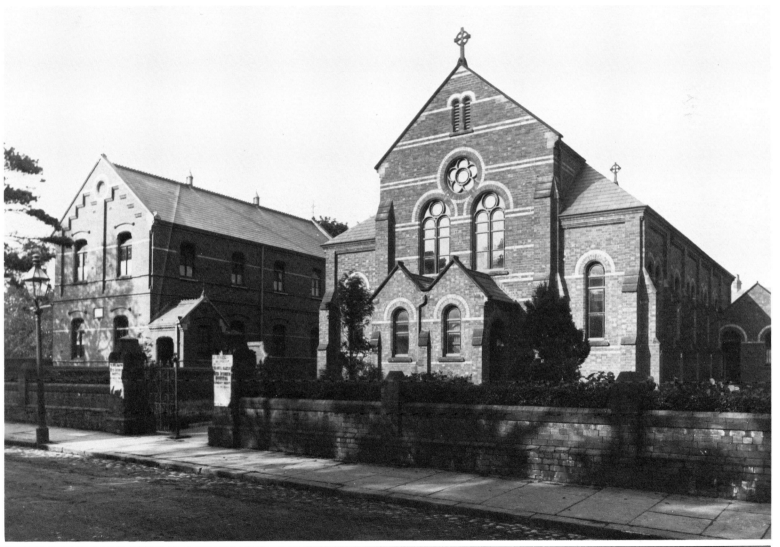

## ORMEAU PARK

Originally the demesne of the early nineteenth-century family house of the Donegalls, this parkland of 175 acres was acquired by the town authorities.[1] It was laid out as Belfast's first public recreation park and opened in 1870.

The architect responsible for designing the park was Timothy Hevey, who showed great promise with buildings such as the Martin Memorial at Shrigley and St Columbcille's Church, Holywood, but who died at the early age of 33.[2] His design for Ormeau combined open parkland to the east with more formal plantings in the middle and wooded walks along the slopes above the Lagan.

This view, looking northwards, shows some of the youthful municipal plantings along the main path. The more mature trees in the background were part of the setting of the Donegall house. Ormeau park now includes a golf course, bowling green and sports tracks. Unfortunately the Australian emus, described in 1884 as being kept in an enclosure in the park, belong to the past.[3]

## BALLYNAFEIGH METHODIST CHURCH, ORMEAU ROAD

This highly original building was designed by the Derry partnership of Taggart Aston and Alfred Forman and completed in 1899.[1]

Contemporary journals refer to the style as 'American Romanesque' and it has some of the robust originality of the work of Henry Hobson Richardson in Chicago. But there is also much of the contemporary style of buildings of entertainment such as Frank Matcham's Grand Opera House.

Nowadays the church is much less exciting. The upper part of the tower and some of the more theatrical skyline finials have been removed. The brickwork panels have been rendered and painted.

## DUNVILLE PARK, AT THE JUNCTION OF GROSVENOR AND FALLS ROADS

Before Queen Victoria's time nobody in Belfast lived more than a few hundred yards away from open countryside but the town's rapid expansion in the second half of the nineteenth century created a sudden need for recreational spaces within the town. Some space for parks was purchased by the town authorities; on other occasions such as at Dunville Park, the town benefited from private generosity.

The park, consisting of 4½ acres, was the gift of R. G. Dunville to the citizens of Belfast. Opened in 1891 it provided and still provides an important open space in a heavily built-up area. The donor also defrayed the cost of laying out the park and providing the fine terracotta fountain, which was designed as a central focus for formal lawns and flower beds.[1]

On the far side, as this view, c.1905, shows, is the Royal Victoria Hospital.

## ROYAL VICTORIA HOSPITAL

Built to replace the Royal Hospital in Frederick Street, this new hospital was opened in 1903 by King Edward VII.[1] It was designed by the Birmingham architects, William Henman and Thomas Cooper, who specialised in hospital buildings.

All the most up-to-date features were incorporated, in particular the revolutionary Plenum System of ventilation, the principle of which had been applied originally for ventilating engine rooms in ships. By this system fresh air was drawn into the building by fans and conveyed along ducts set in the walls. In this way drafts were eliminated as there were no open windows and at the same time there was a continuous change of air. The traditional plan of large detached pavilions, several storeys high, was rejected in favour of a continuous block design to give full advantage to the new ventilation system.

All the wards were on the same level, a series of self-contained units running side by side from the main corridor and looking out on gardens. The view of the wards, c.1906, shows the louvred ventilator shafts above each service tower. The tall buildings in the background are administrative blocks.

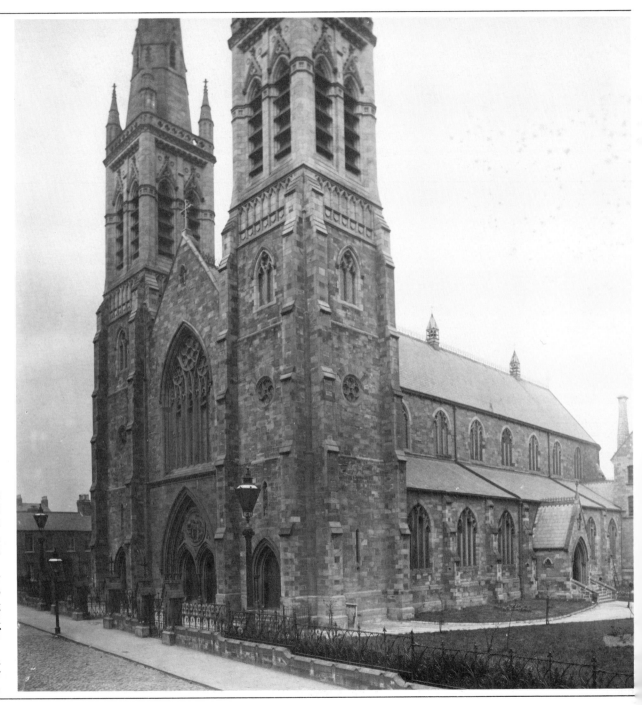

## ST PETER'S CATHOLIC PRO-CATHEDRAL, DERBY STREET, FALLS ROAD

St Peter's was begun in 1860 to designs by Fr Jeremiah Ryan McAuley, a young Belfast architect who had been ordained in 1858 and then become chaplain to the Convent of Mercy on the Crumlin Road.[1] In 1862 he departed to study at the University of Salamanca, possibly for health reasons, and responsibility for the building passed to John O'Neill.

St Peter's was finished and dedicated in 1866, by which time Fr McAuley was back in Belfast serving as a curate; he continued to design churches, notably at Saul, Co. Down, and at Ballycastle during a spell as a curate in the Glens of Antrim.[2] In 1871 he was appointed Administrator of St Peter's but died only two years later at the age of forty-two.

In 1886 spires were added to the already prominent twin towers. A major work of the gothic revival in Belfast, St Peter's is a sparely adorned Victorian translation of a great mediaeval French cathedral.

## FALLS PARK, FALLS ROAD

This park of 45 acres became a recreation area by accident. Originally it was part of the land bought by the town commissioners in the 1860s for a new municipal graveyard. A section was put aside for catholic burials but the catholic bishop, Patrick Dorrian, and the commissioners could not agree on certain rights over the area.

The outcome was that Bishop Dorrian obtained land at Milltown for a catholic cemetery and the land was developed as a public park. It opened in 1878.[1] Is the figure on the right the park-keeper with his top hat, brass buttons and bright boots?

## ST MARY'S COLLEGE AND ST DOMINIC'S COLLEGE, FALLS ROAD

Designed by John O'Shea and E. J. Byrne, St Mary's college as seen on the left, was opened in 1900 to provide teacher training for catholic women teachers.[1] The college was a fashionable mixture of several historic styles.

The gothic chapel, added in 1902, is linked to the main block by a battlemented corridor and the tower over the front door also has battlements although its lower openings are classical, as are most of the windows on the principal block. Nevertheless this also has buttresses, a castle-style canted bay window, and gable parapets which shows a slight tendency towards a Baroque wriggle. Even the fine entrance gates have pedestrian side arches which may be regarded as minor Roman triumphs.

The building to-day has not changed greatly from this view although there is now a new link section between the chapel and the main block. In 1982 the college was amalgamated with St Joseph's College. St Dominic's College (now High School) and run by the Dominican Order is adjacent to St Mary's and is seen here on the right. The architect of St Dominic's was John O'Neill and it was built in the early 1870s.[2]

## PROVINCIAL BANK, HERCULES PLACE, AND ROYAL AVENUE

There is no better illustration of the Victorian City Fathers' attempt to improve the environment and dignity of Belfast than the demolition during 1878 and 1880 of Hercules Place and Street, a narrow way traditionally used as butchers' shambles, and the substitution of the straight lines and grand regular façades of Royal Avenue.

The view on the left shows Hercules Place at the top of Hercules Street, photographed c.1877. The only building here which survives the new development is the Provincial Bank.[1] Designed in the high eclectic style of W. J. Barre it was unfinished at the time of his death in

1867 and was completed under the direction of Turner and Williamson.[2]

The view on the right was taken c.1907 and shows the effect of the changes. Beyond the bank, the next building on the left is the Reform Club with its circular turret and cupola set above the corner door. Officially opened in 1885 the club was designed by the firm of Maxwell and Tuke of Manchester, although the actual construction was supervised by W. H. Lynn.[3] The building beyond with the even higher cupola is the Grand Central Hotel.

## ROYAL AVENUE AND CASTLE JUNCTION

The southern end of Royal Avenue led into Castle Place and so was part of Castle Junction. All the trams, both horse-drawn and electric, ran from this junction. Development of the tramway system was crucial for the growth of Belfast because it allowed people to travel far from their homes to places of work or the central shopping area. The first horse-drawn trams ran in 1872 for the Belfast Street Tramway Company which by the late 1890s had over 1000 horses in use.[1]

In 1904 the service was taken over by the corporation and the sytem was converted to electricity; the last horse tram ran on 5 December 1905. The first electric trams, as seen in this photograph, c.1906, were open-topped but from 1907 vehicles with top covers were introduced and the earlier models were converted to this style. The maximum fare in 1906 was 2d, which remained in operation until the middle of the First World War.[2]

## ROYAL AVENUE, LOOKING NORTHWARDS

This view of Royal Avenue, c.1895, shows the way the new thoroughfare was carefully planned.

The whole site was bought by the town council and leased for development under rigid controls. All the buildings are the same height, apart from the occasional cupola, and they have cornices at a standard level. Most of the premises on the far side of the street, as seen here, were constructed between 1880 and 1885. The third block down was the water commissioners' office, opened in 1883 and built in a classical style from plans by W. J Fennell.[1]

Some of the these buildings, such as Fennell's, have been demolished but Royal Avenue still retains its straight lines. Many fine Victorian façades remain above the modern shop fronts.

ROYAL AVENUE, BELFAST. .W.L.

## GRAND CENTRAL HOTEL, ROYAL AVENUE

This hotel was one of the last buildings to be constructed in Royal Avenue. While most of the rest of the street had been built by 1885, the Grand Central Hotel was not erected until the early 1890s.[1]

The delay seems to have been caused by hopes which were not fulfilled that the site might serve as part of a grand central railway terminus extending into Smithfield, similar to the Central Station in New York.[2] The hotel which eventually appeared was Belfast's largest and most luxurious, with over 200 bedrooms plus numerous suites of apartments.

From the names of the shops on the ground floor we can tell that this photograph was taken c.1895. The building survived as a first-class hotel until the late 1960s when it was closed. For a time it housed army personnel, but it has now been renovated for civilian use, although not as an hotel.

## DRAWING ROOM, GRAND CENTRAL HOTEL

The 1911 illustrated hand-book for the hotel gives a good picture of the facilities on offer.[1]

For the convenience of visitors, omnibuses, 'with hotel porters in uniform', attended the arrival and departure of all trains and steamers. The hotel was lighted throughout by electricity and there were lifts to all floors. Beside the usual well-furnished dining and drawing rooms, (such as that shown here) there were smoking rooms, a writing room and a billiard room. Private sitting rooms cost from 7s.6d.to 15s. per day while for a double bedroom the tariff ran from 6s. upwards.

There were extras: 'attendance' was 1s.6d. per day, and 'hot or cold bath in bedroom' was 1s., a 'hip or sponge bath in bedroom' cost only 6d. and a fire in one's room ran to 1s.6d per day and 1s per night. Visitors' servants were also accommodated: 'board in the stewards' room' was 5s. per day and a bedroom was 3s.

## GENERAL POST OFFICE, ROYAL AVENUE

We can tell now that this view was shot *c.*1890 because the Grand Central Hotel in the centre distance has not yet been completed. The General Post Office on the right was opened in August 1886.[1] It was built of Dungannon stone and the architect was J. H. Owen of the Office of Public Works, who was also Charles Lanyon's brother-in-law. This building still stands but unfortunately its original design has been altered by a large new entrance at the front.

Beside the G.P.O. in the photograph are the premises of the Association for the Employment of the Industrious Blind (founded 1871) which served as workshops for the blind and a show room for their products as well as a library of braille books. Designed by Godfrey Ferguson, the building was completed in 1882.[2] Destroyed by fire in 1908, it was rebuilt the following year to different designs by Henry Seaver.[3]

## ROYAL AVENUE

The last section of Royal Avenue, seen here *c.*1895, turned sharply through North Street and ran along what was formerly John Street to the beginning of York Street.

On the right we can observe another branch of Forster Green, completed in 1884.[1] On the left there is a row of shops and offices, also built in the 1880s, after which stands the handsome classical building of the Belfast Free Library (now the Central Library) in the centre of the view.[2] The library, run by the corporation, housed a lending and reference department, magazine room and museum and art gallery. Opened in 1888, this public building was designed by W. H. Lynn.

Beyond the library are the offices of the *Belfast Telegraph* of 1886, designed by Henry Seaver in a style described as 'a free treatment of the classic period'; contemporary opinion considered it to have 'the most imposing exterior of any newspaper office in Ireland'.[3] The opinion of rival papers around the corner is not recorded.

## YORK STREET, AT THE JUNCTION WITH ROYAL AVENUE AND DONEGALL STREET

Unlike Royal Avenue, York Street was already a long-established thoroughfare when this photograph was taken c.1906.

It was developed in the first half of the nineteenth century but by the 1900s many of the Georgian dwellings in the street had been replaced with commercial and industrial buildings. Gallaher's colossal tobacco factory and the York Street Spinning Mill were both located here.[1]

This end of York Street was very badly damaged in the blitz.

## ST ANNE'S CHURCH AND CATHEDRAL

The old parish church of St Anne, built at Lord Donegall's expense, was completed in 1776 to designs by Francis Hiorne of Warwick.[1] Its fine classical design included Belfast's earliest Roman portico, and a tall tower and cupola. Even before Belfast passed to city status, the growing Church of Ireland population wished for a cathedral. However, the cathedral was not begun until the end of the century. The architect chosen was Sir Thomas Drew, with W. H. Lynn consulting.[2] Drew's 'massive brooding and impressive'[3] Romanesque nave was begun around the old church from which at first only the tower was removed; eventually services were interrupted for only six months.

The photograph below, showing the newly completed nave is interesting; the column capitals are not yet carved; to the left is the pulpit, designed by Sir George Gilbert Scott in 1863, which was a present from Westminster Abbey; and the brick screen wall at the east end incorporates a classical archway and pediment, as well as late-Georgian memorials, suggesting that at this stage part of the old church was still intact. In spite of many delays and difficulties work has continued on the cathedral throughout this century; the east end was completed in 1981.

## YORK STREET

These two views, *c.*1906, show the north end of York Street, approaching the Midland (previously the Belfast and Northern Counties) Railway Station.

The photograph to the right illustrates how many smaller streets, with long rows of industrial housing, ran onto this main thoroughfare. In spite of the shop-front of the Elephant Tea House, the large houses on the immediate left with divided sash windows were obviously built in the early nineteenth century.

The tall terrace of shops with dwellings at the far side, close to the station, seen clearly in the left-hand photograph, belong to the second half of the century.

## BELFAST AND NORTHERN COUNTIES RAILWAY STATION

Train services to the north of the country from Belfast began in 1848 when the Belfast-Ballymena line was opened. The company responsible acquired other companies in Counties Antrim and Londonderry, and in 1860 was named the Belfast and Northern Counties Railway. The Midland Railway took over the B.N.C.R. in 1903 and the company was renamed the Midland Railway (Northern Counties Committee).

The fine classical terminus at York Street with its double-decker portico was built originally in 1848 and extended in 1873-5. Changes in the 1890s involved the building of the clock tower, the hotel facing Whitla Street (see p.70) and various stores.[1] In addition to hotel facilities the hotel had telegraph offices and a coffee stand for the public (which is now at the Ulster Folk and Transport Museum) as well as "locomotive departmental dining-rooms".[2]

During the air raid of 1941 much of the station was destroyed, but the part which survived was finally demolished only in 1977. These two views were taken c.1900. The row of vehicles in front of the station, on the left, consists of outside or jaunting cars except for the covered cab known as a Clarence. The view on the right gives a good idea of the skill with which paving square sets were laid; the larger bands of stone indicated pedestrian crossings.

## ST PATRICK'S CATHOLIC CHURCH, DONEGALL STREET

Timothy Hevey and Mortimer Thompson were the architects of St Patrick's, which was completed in 1878,[1] and is seen here *c.*1900. The original St Patrick's, Belfast's second Roman Catholic church, was begun in 1810 and consecrated in 1815; its architect Patrick Davis produced a building which was traditional classical in layout but gothic in detail.[2] Doing this he established a mediaeval identity for catholic churches which was to last through the century. Unlike those in Dublin, Belfast's late-Georgian neo-classical churches are invariably protestant and usually presbyterian.

By 1874 when the present church was begun on the site of the old one, a more full-blooded mediaevalism was in vogue. The Romanesque revival style of St Patrick's is at its most effective where the tower and spire soar over the street. Its neighbours are much older. To the right is St Patrick's School, a fine example of early gothic revival built in 1828.[3] The school became part of the national school system in the 1830s, and from the mid 1860s until its recent closure it was run by the Christian Brothers.

Left of the church is the parochial house, formerly a bishop's palace. It is probable that this house and those beside it were built in the 1820s.

## VICTORIA BARRACKS, NORTH QUEEN STREET

Military barracks were erected in this area in the late eighteenth century. The original accommodation, however, was greatly increased in 1883 when two new blocks of buildings were constructed under the Cardwell scheme for modernisation of the army.

According to the 1909 Belfast directory, the barracks accommodated 10 officers and 182 soldiers and there were quarters for 32 married soldiers and their families. When required, 1000 men could be garrisoned here and in times of emergency a further 3000 soldiers might be housed under canvas.[1]

This view shows the 1883 barracks buildings with one of the earlier buildings in the background on the right and the parade ground in front. The Artillery Flats now stand on the site of the Victoria Barracks.

### CLIFTON STREET

This view, *c.*1906, looks in the opposite direction from the picture of the churches on the right.

The statue of the Rev. Hugh Hanna is just visible in the middle of Carlisle Circus in the distance.[1] The fine row of chambers on the left is a late-Victorian mixture with oriel windows from England, stepped gables from Flanders, curved Baroque gables from France, and above the Italianate classical Orange Hall, King William III from Holland.

Both the Orange Hall (1889) and the block on the rear side of it with urn finials (1891) were designed by William Batt.[2] The equestrian statue is by Harry Hems of Exeter.[3]

### CARLISLE CIRCUS AND CLIFTON STREET

The gothic revival in church building, because of its association with Pugin, the Oxford Movement and Roman Catholicism, was adopted slowly and with great circumspection by Belfast's non-conformists. Then in the welter of church building which accompanied the disestablishment of the Church of Ireland in 1871, gothic became recognised as an acceptable protestant (if still episcopalian) option. Gradually presbyterians and later methodists, began to use pointed windows and doors, buttresses, finials, towers and spires.

There can be few better demonstrations of how complete the gothic triumph was during the last third of the nineteenth century than this view. On the left is St Enoch's Presbyterian Church erected in 1871-2 to designs by Anthony Jackson.[1] On the right is the Carlisle Memorial Methodist Church, completed 1875 by James Carlisle, a prominent Belfast building contractor, in memory of his son; here the architect was W. H. Lynn.[2]

The gas lamp on the right of the view, in the centre of Carlisle Circus, was replaced with a statue of the Rev. Hugh Hanna in 1894.[3] The Orange Hall in Clifton Street, with the equestrian statue of King Billy on the top,[4] was built in 1889 and its neighbour in 1891 (see opposite). Clearly, then, this photograph was taken 1892-3.

MEMORIAL CHURCHES. BELFAST 2673. W.L

MATER INFIRMORUM HOSPITAL, CRUMLIN ROAD

This hospital was completed in 1900 to designs by W. J. Fennell.[1] Run by the Sisters of Mercy, it replaced another hospital on the opposite side of the Crumlin Road. It was built on the pavilion system with a number of large blocks.

The general style of the hospital is 'institutional Tudor' with shouldered gables, battlements, depressed arches with mouldings linked as string courses, yet resolutely symmetrical. Notice the flat roofs of some of the buildings. Early advertisements for the hospital show hospital beds and patients on the roofs.

On the hoarding at the front of the hospital, seen here c.1906, there is an advertisement for the annual excursion of the Ancient Free Gardeners (a friendly society) to Bundoran at a cost of 3s.6d.

## BELFAST ROYAL ACADEMY, CLIFTONVILLE ROAD

The Academy was originally in Academy Street beside St Anne's church. This new building on much more spacious grounds was constructed to designs by Young and Mackenzie.[1]

Robert Young was himself an Academy boy from a family with Scottish origins who went on to study engineering in Glasgow. He would have been well aware that the Academy was based on the Scottish academies and, although his design owes much to Queen's College (see p.44), which was designed when Young was a junior in Lanyon's office, the Academy also has towers and corbelled turrets which give it a Scottish baronial flavour.

The building was opened in 1880.

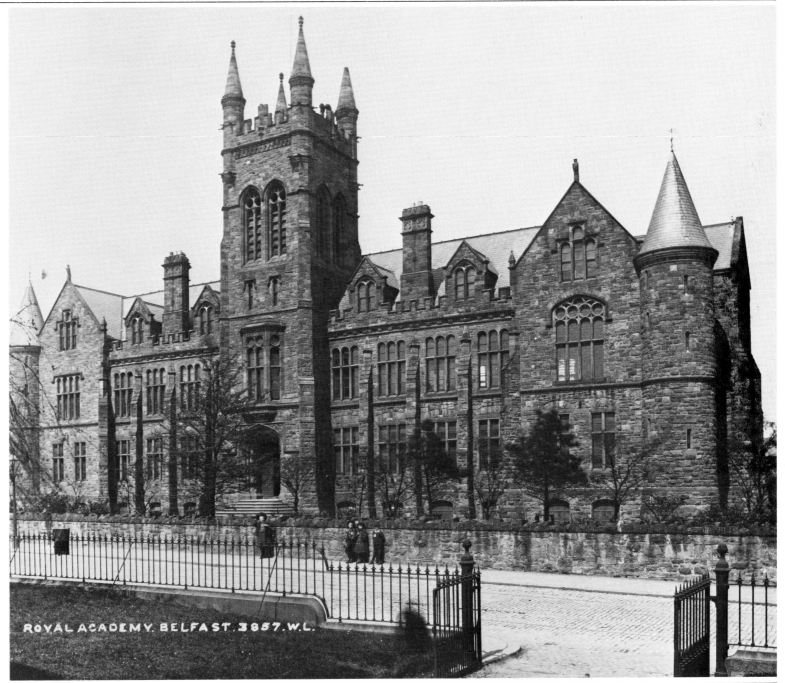

ROYAL ACADEMY. BELFAST. 3857. W.L.

## DUNCAIRN GARDENS

New areas of dwellings were developed on the outskirts of Belfast to keep pace with the rapid population growth. From the early nineteenth century, streets of industrial housing as well as of more substantial terrace houses were built in north Belfast, between the Antrim Road and North Queen Street. But this development was not uniform and some private residences with parkland survived.[1]

A good example was the 34 acre estate and gardens of Belfast solicitor Adam Macrory where a new road of residences, called Duncairn Gardens, was built between 1881 and the late 1890s.[2] It ran from the Antrim Road to North Queen Street. The houses here are, as a consequence, newer than the surrounding dwellings.

The top section of the terrace of houses on the left was destroyed by bombing during the war, but the shops have survived. This photograph is dated c.1906. The bulk of Belfast housing was constructed in the late nineteenth and early twentieth centuries when certain basic standards had already become law. This meant that housing in the city compared well to other industrial centres where development had been earlier. Of course there were areas in Belfast built before the regulations were introduced and these late Victorian and Edwardian houses have measured up badly to twentieth century standards.[3]

## STEAM TRAM, ON THE ANTRIM ROAD AT CHICHESTER PARK

Trams from the centre of Belfast on the Antrim Road route ran only as far as Chichester Park. Opening in July 1882, the Cavehill and Whitewell Tramway Company ran a service by steam tramway from Chichester Park to Glengormley.

During 1891-5 horsetrams also operated on this line and from 1895 the system was worked entirely by horses until electrification of the system in 1908.[1] This view, taken *c*.1890, shows one of the steam-engines which hauled a double deck, open-top trailer. The horse-drawn tram in the background is probably starting a journey back to the city centre.

## JUBILEE AVENUE AND THE ENTRANCE TO ALEXANDRA PARK

This avenue was laid down in the year of Queen Victoria's golden jubilee. However, while the smaller terrace houses on the right in the shade were built in 1887, the much larger houses on the left with more spacious gardens were not built until the early 1890s. This photograph is an unusual one in the Lawrence collection as it seems to be the only view of Belfast suburban houses which was taken; even this was probably accidental because the main purpose of the view was to show the entrance to Alexandra Park. The man with the ice-cream barrows was already an attraction at the gates.

## ALEXANDRA PARK

Situated between Antrim Road, Shore Road and Limestone Road, Alexandra Park was opened by the corporation in 1887, following extensive work which was carried out as part of a relief works scheme for the unemployed. It received its title in 1885 after the visit of the Prince and Princess of Wales to Belfast in that year. Originally the park was only 10 acres in extent, but a further 10 acres were added in 1908.[1]

This view is westward. The gabled house in the distance with the glass house is the park-keeper's lodge at the Jubilee Avenue gates. These children are all well turned-out for their visit to the park—but notice the barefooted children at the extreme left of the photograph. Out of sight to the left is the lake. Little has changed in a century except the behaviour of the visitors, and the size of the trees, now approaching glorious maturity. The narrow, lower glen was recently replanted.

## CAVE HILL ROAD

This view shows the city reaching into the country in late Victorian times. On the right are thoroughly urban terraced middle-class villas with decent if undistinguished brickwork and fine front railings and gates. Across the road open fields reach almost up to the newly planted slopes of Cave Hill, without building interruption.

In the distance can be seen Belfast Castle. What this picture does not reveal is that on the immediate left behind the railings there ran the track of the Cavehill Railway Company. This line, a gravity-fed tramway system, carried limestone from quarries on Cave Hill to the docks for export. The photograph is dated *c.*1895 because it appeared in *Views of Belfast and the County Down* (Dublin, 1897).

## ENTRANCE GATES TO FORTWILLIAM PARK

Fortwilliam Park was probably Belfast's most exclusive suburban park at the turn of the century. The park, which ran from the Antrim Road to the Shore Road, contained large detached residences with substantial gardens. Fine gates stood at each end. Both these views were probably taken *c.*1890.

The gateways were designed by William Barre (1830-67), a year or two before his early death.[1]. They neatly represent the two main historical styles than competing for popularity. Above, at Antrim Road, the stone piers are modified gothic canopies with pointed arches and other mediaeval decorations. By contrast, at the Shore Road the style is classical, and pedestrian access is by miniature Roman triumphal arches. Both central piers have now gone.

### CAVE HILL

Look up from the streets of the city,
Look high beyond tower and mist,
What hand of what Titan sculptor,
Smote the crags on the mountain vast.

Made when the world was fashioned,
Meant with the world to last,
That glorious face of the sleeper,
That slumbers above Belfast.
*From 'Mountain shapes' by Alice Milligan.*[1]

These well turned out Edwardians are in front of one of the caves (hence the name) situated in the face of Cave Hill. This view looks north east towards Mossley, whiteabbey and the Knockagh.

### BELFAST CASTLE

The Chichesters, who received the title of Donegall, were the landlords of Belfast although by the mid-nineteenth century they retained little direct control over the town and had dissipated most of their family fortune.

In 1857, however, Harriet, only surviving child of the third Marquis of Donegall, married the son and heir of the seventh Earl of Shaftesbury.[1] Thanks to the Shaftesbury money, the Marquis of Donegall was able to commission Lanyon, Lynn and Lanyon to build a new residence on the slopes of Cave Hill. John Lanyon was the partner responsible.[2] Completed in 1870 the building was in the grand Scottish baronial style. It contained 30 bedrooms, a salon and drawing, morning, dining and billiard rooms as well as extensive servants' quarters;[3] in 1901 Lord Shaftesbury had 19 domestic servants.[4]

In 1934 the ninth Lord Shaftesbury presented the grounds and castle to the corporation. This photograph was taken after 1894 when an outside staircase was constructed at the back of the building.

# PORT
## AND
# HARBOUR

## THE HARBOUR OFFICE, CORPORATION SQUARE

Although well situated at the mouth of the Lagan, Belfast did not have a good natural harbour. Development of port facilities was therefore essential for the growth of Belfast in the nineteenth and early twentieth centuries.

This work was carried out largely by the commissioners of the harbour board, a body founded in 1847 which took control of the entire docks and harbour area[1] (previously, members of the ballast board had exercised influence over the port). Their headquarters at the Harbour Office, built on the site of William Ritchie's original shipyard, was opened in 1854 to a design by the harbour engineer, George Smith.[2]

This photograph was taken after 1895, when the building was greatly enlarged in a similar Italianate style by W. H. Lynn;[3] all that is visible of Smith's building in this view is the central roof gazebo, and possibly part of the façade on the right.

## CLARENDON DOCK

Opened in 1851, Clarendon Dock, built by the harbour board to accommodate the expanding foreign trade, was the first of a number of new docks on the County Antrim waterfront.[1]

St Joseph's church (designed by Timothy Hevey, who died in 1878, and completed by Mortimer Thompson 1881[2]) and various shops and public houses are in the background; this was part of the area known as Sailorstown. To the left there are several yachts and behind these a large sailing trawler. In the middle of the view there is a trading ketch while to the right is the stern of a schooner or ketch.

This photograph was taken probably in the early 1890s by which time the dock, with its shallow basin, was used for less important trade such as the export of limestone. The Clarendon Dock has now been filled in.

## THE CUSTOM HOUSE

The building of the Belfast Custom House in the 1850s was a sign of the growth in importance of trade to and from the port. The next half century witnessed an even greater expansion of business. In 1905 nearly 60% of customs revenue received at all Irish ports came from Belfast. In only two other ports in the British Isles in the same year was there more customs revenue collected than in Belfast.[1]

The Custom House, opened in 1857, is often regarded as Charles Lanyon's finest achievement, but probably owes much to W. H. Lynn who became Lanyon's partner in 1854.[2] Whoever designed it, the building is Belfast's grandest example of the adaptation of the style of Italian Renaissance merchants' buildings to Victorian mercantile purposes.

The building was designed to hold the Post Office as well; hence the extra set of steps on the near wing which was probably removed when the new G.P.O. was opened in 1886 (see p.66).

## SPENCER DOCK

Opened in 1872, the Spencer Dock provided not only additional quay space but also deeper water which was now required for the increasingly larger vessels which were using the port.

On the left of the photograph there is a wooden barque, North American built, which was probably bringing in a cargo of wood. Extensive timber storage accommodation was provided at the Spencer Dock. Facilities were also afforded for the floating storage of timber in three ponds of forty-four acres in area.[1] On the right of the view is the *Bangor Castle*, an iron paddle steamer, built in 1864. This vessel was used between Belfast and Bangor from 1877 until 1894, when she was sold to a Plymouth firm.[1]

The Spencer Dock lies on the north west side of the harbour, on the County Antrim shore: it is now called Barnett Dock.

QUEEN'S BRIDGE

The Queen's Bridge was built in 1842 on the site of the old Long Bridge, and named in honour of the young Victoria; design and supervision were the responsibility of the county surveyors of Antrim (Charles Lanyon) and Down (John Frazer).[1] It stands at the head of the harbour and also marks the end of the Lagan Navigation which stretched from Lough Neagh.

The photograph on the left, taken probably in the late 1870s, of the upriver side of the bridge, shows the canal quay on the left hand side while in the centre is a steam-tug, used for towing canal lighters (barges).

The photograph on the right, looking from the canal quay, shows the bridge after the cantilever widening carried out by J. C. Bretland in 1885-6.[2]. Both photographs show the masts of coal schooners on the far right-hand side of the bridge.

RIVER VIEW

Taken from the Queen's Bridge and looking towards the sea, *c.* 1900, this photograph shows how the cross-channel steamers were docked to the left along the Donegall Quay while the sailing colliers were to be found on the right along the Queen's Quay. The tonnage of vessels using the port stood at nearly 800,000 tons in 1857 but fifty years later the figure had increased more than threefold.[1]

During this period the existing quays were renewed and extended and additional docks were built to cope with the increase in trade. Immediately in front of this view is a Bangor steamer, tied up beside a jetty which extended out from the bridge for the Belfast-Bangor service.

QUEEN'S QUAY AND RAILWAY STATION

The Queen's Quay provided the principal dock facilities on the County Down side of the harbour, which was otherwise dominated by shipbuilding yards. This view shows a busy scene at the quay in front of the terminus of the Belfast and County Down Railway (rebuilt in 1892).

Many different forms of transport, for passengers and cargo, can be seen in the street and along the dockside. Just in front of the station a low slung cart (a dray) with ramps for loading goods may be observed. In 1901 nearly 3000 men in Belfast were employed as carters, carriers, carmen and draymen.[1]

This photograph was taken before 1895 when major additions were made to the Harbour Office seen here across the Lagan.

## QUEEN'S QUAY

This photograph was taken outside the Belfast and County Down Railway Station and shows a row of jarveys and jaunting cars waiting for passengers. Was it shot the same day as the view on p. 95? Beyond the vehicles can be seen the masts of colliers drawn up at the quayside.

By the last quarter of the nineteenth century, the Queen's Quay had become the main area for the discharge of coal. Because speed was of little advantage in the transport of coal it continued to be carried by sailing colliers much later than other cargoes. The arrival of 40 of these small ships a day in Belfast was normal in the 1870s.[1]

By the 1880s, over half of the colliers arriving were steamers, but the sailing colliers continued to operate until the First World War.

## DISCHARGING COAL, QUEEN'S QUAY

The ship in the foreground is the 182 ton wooden brigantine, the *Regal*. She was one of two ships owned by M. Crean of 2 Queen's Quay who was engaged in the coal trade. Built in 1865 at Prince Edward Island, Canada, the *Regal* was no longer registered by 1899.[1] The coal was brought mostly from the north west of England but sometimes it came from Cardiff; Welsh coal was best for railway and steamship engines.

On the left of the photograph are various schooners and brigantines while on the right are two cross-channel steamers with the Custom House in the background (see p.92). The railway lines enabled the coal to be transported swiftly to any part of the province.

QUAY'S, BELFAST. W L.

## P.S. ADDER AND S.S. VIPER

The view on the left was taken at the mouth of the Clarendon Dock and shows the *P.S. Adder* with the Harland and Wolff Shipyard in the background. The *Adder* was engaged on the daylight run from Belfast to Scotland between 1890 and 1906; Gourock was the Scottish terminus for this service until Ardrossan came into use in 1893. The *S.S. Viper*, as seen on the right, replaced the *Adder* on the Belfast-Ardrossan trip in 1906.[1]

In that year there were daily trips not only to Ardrossan but also to Liverpool, Fleetwood, Heysham and Glasgow. There were journeys three nights a week to Dublin, Barrow, Ayr and Bristol. Once a week sailings occurred to London, Plymouth, Southampton and Stockton on Tees. Behind the *Viper* the skyline is filled with the silhouette of a great ocean liner taking shape in the shipyard.

## BANGOR BOAT TERMINUS AND STEAMER

The Belfast to Bangor excursion, by paddle steamer, was an extremely popular outing for Belfast people in the half century before the First World War. This journey reached its peak of popularity in the 1880s and 1890s when as many as eight round trips a day were on offer during the summer season. The Belfast and County Down Railway entered the business in 1893, offering return fares of 1s.6d. and 1s.[1]

This view on the left of the terminus is taken from Donegall Quay looking over the cutting for the railway line which crossed the Lagan at this point to link up with the County Down side. From the name of the vessels on the advertising hoarding it is clear that this view was taken between 1894 and 1899. The *Slieve Donard* was the first vessel owned by the railway company and it ran on Belfast Lough during this period.[2]

The view on the right shows one of the paddle-steamers setting out on its journey. The Bangor Boat became the subject of a Belfast children's street song which was still being sung in the 1950s.[3]

*The Bangor Boat's away,*
*It hadn't time to stay*
*One in a rush, two in a rush,*
*The Bangor Boat's away.*

## THE JETTY AND THE *P.S. SLIEVE BEARNAGH*

The view on the left shows the *P.S. Slieve Bearnagh* arriving at the Bangor jetty which extended from the Queen's Bridge. This vessel was the second ship operated by the Belfast and County Down Railway on the trip to Bangor. Built in 1894, she ran on the route until 1912. After being sold to a Dundee company, she was requisitioned as a minesweeper during the First World War and was scrapped in the early 1920s.

The view on the right shows the *Slieve Bearnagh* tied up at the jetty. The regular excursion to Bangor ceased in 1915 and while intermittent attempts were made to continue the service up to 1949, the journey failed to attract again the large numbers which had formerly enjoyed the event.[1]

# LINEN
# AND SHIPS

## BROOKFIELD MILL, CRUMLIN ROAD

On the original negative this building is incorrectly described as a linen factory. It is in fact a linen mill where spinning occurred, that is where flax was turned into thread. A factory was where the thread was woven into cloth.

The Brookfield Linen Company, owners of this mill, began operations in the 1860s because of the rise in demand for linen owing to the American Civil War which badly disrupted the manufacture of cotton.[1] The mill continued in operation until the early 1950s;[2] the building still stands and is part of an enterprise zone.

## INTERIOR OF EWART'S MILL, CRUMLIN ROAD

This photograph shows men, known as roughers, engaged in sorting flax. The scutched flax had already been combed out and heckled before this stage, which involved selecting the good flax to be used for fine yarn. The men were standing by the windows to gain maximum light for their work.

This stage was one of the most unhealthy in linen manufacture because the fibre dust often affected the workers' lungs. The hot and humid atmosphere found in other parts of the mills and factories also were harmful to employees' health.[1] William Ewart and Sons had commenced business as cotton manufacturers. Their new flax spinning mill on the Crumlin Road was built in 1865.[2]

SPINNING FACTORY. BELFAST 2412 W. L.

## YORK STREET MILL

This view of part of the York Street Mill was taken at the junction of Henry Street and North Queen Street. Founded by the Mulholland family, the firm had originally been involved in mechanised cotton spinning and was the first to build in 1830 a mill in York Street for flax spinning. This led quickly to the mechanisation of flax spinning throughout the Belfast region.

By the early 1900s the York Street Flax Spinning Company was the largest spinning mill in the world and employed almost 5000 operatives in its York Street mill.[1] The census report of 1901 reveals that in that year 29,302 people, over two-thirds of them women or girls, were engaged in the manufacture of linen in Belfast. Part of this building survives despite severe bomb damage in 1941.[2] The York Street Mill closed down in 1962.[3]

## REELING ROOM IN EWART'S MILL, CRUMLIN ROAD

After the yarn had been spun it was then brought to the reeling room. This view of the reeling room at the top of Ewart's Mill shows the final stage in the spinning where the mill girls reeled the yarn from bobbins to hanks (or bundles) of 60,000 yards in length. At the beginning of the twentieth century, the average working week at the local mills and factories was 55 hours.

Women's wages ranged between 9s. and 12s. per week, except for skilled weavers, who could earn 18s. To view this in proper perspective, it should be noted that in 1905 tea cost 2s. per lb, bacon 8d.-10d. per lb, and eggs 1s.2d. per dozen. A typical house rent was 3s.6d. per week.[1] This photograph appeared in *Views of Belfast and the County Down* (Dublin, 1897) and so can be dated c.1895.

## WEAVING ROOM IN LINEN FACTORY

This photograph of a weaving room in an unidentified linen factory shows damask cloth being woven. Workers stood between the looms. Jacquard cards which were used in the weaving of figured fabrics are seen above the machines. In this instance the cloth is being wefted with bleached yarn so that bleaching of the finished cloth will be unnecessary. In the case of certain fine linens bleaching occurred before the weaving stage but more often it did not take place until afterwards.

## LINEN BLEACH GREEN

There is no indication on the plate where this photograph was taken, but it is included in the catalogue among the Belfast material, and so it was probably somewhere near Belfast. These bleach greens around the city were usually owned by Belfast factories for the bleaching of their cloth.

This view shows the linen cloth, already boiled, lying in the fields to allow natural bleaching from the sun and elements. The linen was normally laid out in webs about 90 yards long and regularly turned to make the bleaching even.

## ROYAL ULSTER WORKS, DUBLIN ROAD

The Royal Ulster Works was the linen warehouse of John Shaw Brown of Edenderry, County Down. This firm specialised in fine linen, principally damask dinner cloths.

The warehouse was where the last stages of manufacture took place. The material was sent from their weaving factory to the bleachworks and then in long webs to the warehouse for cutting, hemming and boxing in wooden crates. Linen towels also were prepared here. Prior to Brown's taking over the building, it had been the property of the prominent printing firm of Marcus Ward and Co., which went bankrupt in 1901.[1]

This mid-Victorian building had a fine front block with an almost ecclesiastical doorway, but the rear exterior was more utilitarian. It was burnt and destroyed in the mid 1970s.

## BEDFORD STREET

In 1902 Bedford Street was described as the headquarters of the linen business.[1] Ewart's warehouse and offices, designed by James Hamilton in 1869,[2] are on the immediate left of this *c.*1900 photograph while beyond there are two other blocks of warehouses and offices. In the vicinity were a large number of such warehouses.

By this period the linen merchants had no formal market centre and it was in and around this street that the main business of buying and selling the finished linen product occurred.[3] On the right is the canopy of the Ulster Hall (see pp38-9), and in the far distance is the present Linen Hall Library (see p.20).

## ALBERT BRIDGE AND QUEEN'S BRIDGE

These two bridges were the main links between the city centre and the busy industrial area of Ballymacarrett to the east. The view on the left, *c.* 1906, of the Queen's Bridge, (see pp. 94-5) gives a good idea of the bustling industrial life in east Belfast. Shipbuilding, ropemaking, distilleries, machine works and many other major industries were located here.

The Albert Bridge collapsed in the 1880s and this view on the right shows the new bridge, designed by J. C. Bretland, the city surveyor, and opened in 1890.[1] Behind the bridge can be seen the 'late baroque' municipal electricity works and offices, designed by Graeme Watt and Frederick Tullock.[2] This power station began operating in 1898 to provide electric lighting in the city and was then extended in 1905 to supply the new electric tram service.[3]

## PILOT OFFICE

These workmen at the Pilot Office are completing a stage in the 8 miles of tramway and railway lines which traversed the docks on both sides of the Lagan. This transport system allowed goods to be transferred from the docks to the railway stations at Queen's Bridge and York Street.

The Pilot Office, best described as a 'collapsed telescope in the Tudor manner', stood at the entrance to Spencer Dock. The cannon were probably trophies from the Crimean War.

In the background are the shipyards of Workman, Clark. This company had begun operations in 1879 and came to lead the way in several areas of shipbuilding; for example it pioneered the development of the refrigerated steamer.[1] By 1917 the company's yards covered 80 acres but the business foundered in 1935.[2]

## FERRY BOAT AT THE QUAYS

This ferry boat is conveying workers between the Abercorn Basin and Donegall Quay. By the 1890s the Belfast Harbour Commissioners ran three of these ferry crossings. The double-ended ferry boats were licensed to carry about 120 persons.[1] By 1917 it was estimated that nearly one and a half million passengers per year were carried by these boats.[2]

This service continued until the early 1930s. Ferry No 5, as seen in this photograph, c.1900, was built in 1899 by the local firm of McIlwaine and MacColl, which was taken over by Workman, Clark in 1893.[3] In the background is the *P.S. Manx Queen* which operated on the service between Barrow and Belfast.

SHIPBUILDING YARDS

This general view on the left is of the Queen's yard, one of the main shipyards in the Harland and Wolff complex on the County Down side of the harbour. It shows stores of steel plates in the centre with a vessel under construction on the right. The steel ramp in the foreground gave workmen access to a ship.

In 1858 Edward Harland acquired the small shipbuilding firm of Robert Hickson. He was joined three years later by G. W. Wolff. In only 40 years the yard expanded from a 3½-acre to a 135-acre site. By 1917 the firm employed between 16,000 and 17,000 men.[1]

The photograph on the right was taken from No. 2 jetty Abercorn basin, adjacent to the Queen's yard. Note how the steel boats are still being constructed in wooden scaffolding. The first boat, the *Salamanca*, has been plated and is due for launching. The other two are still just in their frames. The *Salamanca* was a vessel of 5870 tons. She was built for the Hamburg-Amerik line and launched in 1906.[2]

## TUG IN DOCK

This wooden-built paddle tug is lying in the Hamilton Graving Dock, which was opened in 1867. It was probably used as a tug boat in Belfast Lough but occasionally would have carried passengers.

The dock had a length of 451 ft. After the dock gates were opened and a ship admitted into the dock, water was expelled by the pumping station on the right. Wooden beams were used to keep the vessel in position. The purpose of the graving dock was to enable repair, survey and maintenance work to be carried out on vessels with ease.

As the size of ships increased so the harbour commissioners built larger graving docks. The Thompson Graving Dock, completed in 1911, was the largest dock of its type in the world.[1]

## NO. 1 JETTY, ABERCORN BASIN

These two ships, the *Ortega* and the *Oronsa*, photographed here 1906, are in the final stages of being fitted out.

On the right are the masting shears which were used for lifting masts and engines. The boxes over the sterns of the two centre ships are latrines for the workers. Both vessels were built for the Pacific Steam Navigation Company and were launched in early 1906. Until the First World War both vessels operated on the Liverpool-West Coast of America mail service.

The *Ortega* achieved sudden fame, when, in September 1914, she was chased by a German cruiser and only escaped when sailing through the Nelson Strait, waters never before navigated by a ship of her draught.[1]

## TEUTONIC

Harland and Wolff were noted builders of advanced and innovative high class passenger ships. The *Teutonic* was designed by Edward Harland in 1880, but was not built until 1887-9.

One of a long series of vessels ordered by the White Star Line, this twin-screwed steel-hulled liner of nearly 10,000 tons could carry over 1300 passengers. The dining saloon could seat 300 at one sitting. Her first passage to New York was in a record time of 6 days 17 hours and 25 minutes. Along with her sister ship, the *Majestic*, the *Teutonic* was built so that she could be quickly converted into an auxiliary cruiser for the Admiralty.

During the First World War the Teutonic was used as an armed merchant cruiser. She was broken up in 1921.[1]

## ALEXANDRA GRAVING DOCK

The Alexandra Graving Dock, designed by Redfern Kelly and T. R. Salmond,[1] was opened in 1889.

This sailing barque with three masts has a steel hull. Vessels such as this dominated the shipping world until the last decades of the nineteenth century. Only in 1882 did the tonnage of new steamships equal the tonnage of new sailing ships in the British Isles.[2] Harland and Wolff built its last sailing ship in the 1890s.

These vessels continued to be used quite widely for long haul, bulk cargoes such as grain from the west coast of the United States or nitrate from South America until the First World War. Even up to 1938 the occasional trading sailing vessel still visited Belfast port.[3]

# SOURCES

THE MAJOR BOOK on Robert French and his work is Kieran Hickey's *The light of other days: Irish life at the turn of the century in the photographs of Robert French* (London, 1973). Another important volume, *Steps and steeples: Cork at the turn of the century* (Dublin, 1981), by Colm Lincoln, studies his photographs of Cork. Many of the pictures of Belfast which French took for his employer were used to illustrate contemporary guide-books. As part of the so-called 'Emerald Isle Series', *Views of Belfast and the County Down* was published by Lawrence in Dublin in 1897; it contained forty-one views of the city, mainly of post-card size. For the work of other photographers in Ulster at the turn of the century, see B. M. Walker, *Shadows on glass: a portfolio of early Ulster photography* (Belfast, 1976).

A number of recently published books give valuable information on the historical development of Belfast. Jonathan Bardon's *Belfast: an illustrated history* (Belfast, 1982) covers well the history of Belfast from earliest days to the present. An important collection of essays on different aspects of the growth of Belfast can be found in J. C. Beckett *et al, Belfast: the making of the city* (Belfast 1982). Sybil Gribbon's *Edwardian Belfast* is a good study of Belfast society in the first decade of the twentieth century. *The changing face of Belfast* (Belfast 1969; 2nd revised edition, 1982) by Noel Nesbitt, is very useful for the changes in Belfast streets over the last two hundred years.

The best account of Belfast's architectural development, which also mentions the careers of the principal architects, is C. E. B. Brett, *Buildings of Belfast 1700-1914* (London 1967). Journals provide much information about Belfast's buildings and general development. *The Dublin Builder*, begun in 1859, which became *The Irish Builder* in 1868, is especially useful (and is now available on microfilm at the Public Record Office of Northern Ireland and elsewhere). London journals, *The Builder, An illustrated weekly magazine for the Drawing-room, the Studio, the Office, the Workshop, and the Cottage*, begun in 1843, and *The Architect*, begun in 1869, are more selectively helpful. Belfast buildings are placed in a wider context in Hugh Dixon's *An introduction to Ulster architecture*, (Belfast 1975) and *Ulster architecture 1800-1900, a catalogue of drawings*, (Belfast 1972).

Right: Falls Road Park (R3410).

# NOTES
## AND PLATE NUMBERS

### ABBREVIATIONS

This list of abbreviations covers titles of books which are used frequently in the notes. Where books are referred to only a few times, the titles are not included here but abbreviated in the text; the full title and date of publication are given in the first citation.

| | |
|---|---|
| Beckett, *Belfast* | J. C. Beckett *et al, Belfast, the making of the city* (Belfast, 1982) |
| *Belfast directory* | *Directory of Belfast and the province of Ulster* (Belfast, 1870-1914) |
| Brett, *Belfast* | C. E. B. Brett, *Buildings of Belfast 1700-1914* (Belfast, 1967) |
| Dixon, *Introduction* | Hugh Dixon, *An introduction to Ulster architecture* (Belfast, 1975) |
| Dixon, *1800-1900* | Hugh Dixon, *Ulster architecture 1800-1900* (Belfast, 1972) |
| *Industries of Ireland* | *Industries of Ireland: part I: Belfast and the towns of the north* (London, 1891) |

### CATALOGUE NUMBERS

The numbers quoted beside the plate titles refer to the catalogue numbers of the photographs in the National Library Lawrence Collection. Abbreviations of the different series titles are:
C—Cabinet, I—Imperial, NS—New Series and R—Royal.

**Front cover.** Donegall Place     I 2672

**Page II.** Castle Place     C 2426

**Page V** Donegall Place R3843.

**Pages VII—IX**
1. Leslie Clarkson, 'The city and the country' in Beckett, *Belfast,* p. 159, (hereafter cited as Clarkson, *City and country*). Population figures from 1851 onwards have come from W. E. Vaughan and A. J. Fitzpatrick (ed.) *Irish historical statistics: population 1821-1971.* (Dublin, 1978), pp 36-7.
2. *McComb's guide to Belfast* (Belfast, 1861), p.4.
3. Clarkson, *City and country*, p. 153.
4. See Kieran Hickey, *The light of other days: Irish life at the turn of the century in the photographs of Robert French* (London, 1973).

**Page XI.** Castle Place     R 318

**Page 2.** Castle Place     I 320
1. There is a view of the original Bank Buildings in S. S. Millin, *Sidelights on Belfast history* (Belfast, 1932), p.22; another in the Ulster Museum is reproduced in Beckett, *Belfast*, p.158.
2. *The Builder*, 1861, p.175; Brett, *Belfast*, p.31.

**Page 3.** Castle Place     R 318
1. Brett, *Belfast*, p. 52; Lynn appears to have been employed by the firm to alter the Bank Buildings since the 1880s; see *Industries of Ireland*, p. 102. For Lynn's career see Hugh Dixon in *Irish Georgian Society Bulletin*, XVII, 1974, pp 25-30.

**Page 4.** Cornmarket     R 5813
1. A. S. Moore, *Belfast today* (Belfast, 1913) p. 44 (hereafter cited as Moore, *Belfast*).
2. *Irish Builder*, 1868, p. 33; for Jackson's career, see Hugh Dixon in *Proceedings of the Belfast Natural History and Philosophical Society*, 1978, pp 23-31.
3. *Dublin Builder*, 1866, p. 133; *Irish Builder*, 1868, pp 144, 159; *The Builder*, 1868, p. 493.

**Page 5.** Theatre Royal, Arthur Square     C 2419
1. The plain appearance of the original theatre may be seen in a mid-19th century coloured 'Marcotype' print in Ulster Museum.
2. *Irish Builder*, 1871, p. 245.
3. John Gray, 'Popular entertainment' in Beckett, *Belfast*, pp 107-10; Catalogue of exhibition on Belfast theatres held in Belfast Central Library: typescript, Belfast Central Library, 1979, p.5.
4. *The Builder*, 1917, p.27; the architect was Bertie Crewe who also designed the Hippodrome, see p. 35.

**Pages 6/7.** High Street     I 319     C 2415
1. *Bombs on Belfast, photographs by Belfast Telegraph*, (Belfast, 1941), unpaginated, turn 4, 5 and 8.

**Page 8.** St George's Church, High Street     I 2678
1. Brett, *Belfast*, p. 13; Dixon, *1800-1900*, p. 16.
2. P. J. Rankin, *Irish building ventures of the Earl Bishop of Derry*, (Belfast, 1972) p.63.

**Page 9.** The National Bank, High Street     R 4410
1. *Irish Builder*, 1897, p. 24; Brett, *Belfast*, pp 46-7.

**Page 10.** The Albert Memorial Clock     I 516
1. *Dublin Builder*, 1865, pp 153, 183, 216. *The Builder*, 1866, p. 273.
2. For Barre's career and the scandalous row surrounding the competition to design the Albert Clock see Durham Dunlop, *The life of W. J. Barre* (Belfast, 1868) (herafter cited as Dunlop, *Barre*), Brett, *Belfast, p. 34, and Dixon, 1800-1900*, p. 27.
3. Brett, *Belfast*, p. 30.

**Page 11.** Ulster Bank Head Office, Waring Street     R 2389
1. *The Builder*, 1858, p. 250; *Dublin Builder*, 1859, pp 134-5.
2. Brett, *Belfast*, pp 29, 37.

**Page 12.** Victoria Street     C 2412
1. See James Williamson's map of Belfast of 1791; an enlargement of the relevant portion is reproduced in Kenneth McNally, *The narrow streets* (Belfast, 1972), p.22.
2. Eileen McCracken, *The Palm House and Botanic Garden, Belfast* (Belfast, 1971), pp 51-3 (hereafter cited as McCracken, *Palm House*).

**Page 13.** The Town Hall, Victoria Street     C 1261
1. *Irish Builder*, 1869, p. 171; Brett, *Belfast*, p. 45; Dixon, *1800-1900*, p. 27.
2. Ulster Museum Art Department

**Pages 14 and 15**. Donegall Place    I 512    NS 2727
1.  Moore, *Belfast*, p. 23.
2.  McLaughlin and Harvey papers, Public Record Office of Northern Ireland (hereafter cited as PRONI), D1898/1/19; Dixon, *1800-1900*, p. 28.
3.  *Industries of Ireland*, p. 41.

**Page 16**. Imperial Hotel, Donegall Place    I 1320
1.  *Irish Builder*, 1868, pp 153, 202; Mr Jury also owned Jury's and Shelbourne Hotels, Dublin, and Imperial Hotel, Cork.
2.  *Industries of Ireland*, p. 75

**Page 17**. Queen's Arcade, Donegall Place    C 2420
1.  Dixon, *1800-1900*, p. 28.
2.  *Industries of Ireland*, p. 139.

**Pages 18 and 19**. Donegall Place    I 323    I 2727
1.  Brett, *Belfast*, p. 37; the bank was demolished in 1965.
2.  See W. A. Maguire *'Lords and landlords—the Donegall Family'*, in Beckett, *Belfast*, p. 28
3.  *Industries of Ireland*, p. 93.

**Page 20**. Donegall Square North    C 1245
1.  *Dublin Builder*, 1864, p. 232.
2.  See John Magee, *The Linen Hall Library and the cultural life of Georgian Belfast* (Belfast, 1982).

**Page 21**. Richardson's Warehouse, Donegall Square North    I 326
1.  *Dublin Builder*, 1866, p. 133; *Industries of Ireland*, p. 68

**Pages 22 and 23**. Robinson and Cleaver, Donegall Square North   I 1998   I 1999
1.  *Irish Builder*, 1888, pp 68-9.
2.  *Industries of Ireland*, pp 78-9.
3.  Brett, *Belfast*, p. 47.

**Pages 24 and 25**. The White Linen Hall, Donegall Square    C 1251    C 1255
1.  Brett, *Belfast*, p. 6; for Mulholland's career see C. E. B. Brett, *Roger Mulholland: architect of Belfast, 1740-1818* (Belfast, 1976).
2.  Robert Esler, *Guide to Belfast, Giant's Causeway and North of Ireland* (Belfast 1884), p. 19 (hereafter cited as Esler, *Belfast*)

**Pages 26 and 27**. The City Hall, Donegall Square    R 2386    R 9253
1.  *The Builder*, 1906, pp 233-5, 248; *A monograph of the City Hall . . . of Belfast illustrated*, (Belfast, 1906).
2.  Brett, *Belfast*, 54; A. Service, *Edwardian architecture* (London, 1975), p. 308.

**Page 28**. Donegall Square East
1.  *Irish Builder*, 1899, p. 213; *The Builder*, 1902, p. 508; Brett, *Belfast*, p. 59.
2.  Brett, *Belfast*, p. 11; Imperial House was designed by Kendrick Edwards, *Irish Builder*, 1937, p. 7.
3.  Brett, *Belfast*, p. 28; Dixon, *1800-1900*, p. 18.

**Page 29**. Scottish Provident Institution, Donegall Square West    R 2368
1.  *The Builder*, 1902, p. 454, and 1903, p. 556; Brett, *Belfast*, pp 58-9.
2.  *Irish Builder*, 1895, p. 211.

**Page 30** Wellington Place    C 1252
1.  *The Builder*, 1858, p. 615; the church was replaced by the Athletic Stores, *Irish Builder*, 1899, p. 140.
2.  *The Architect*, 1877, p. 161.

3.  Brett, *Belfast*, p. 12; Hugh Dixon, *Soane and the Belfast Academical Institution* (Dublin, 1976); Dixon, *1800-1900*, p. 21.
4.  Brett, *Belfast*, p. 10.

**Page 31**. College Square East    C 1248
1.  The statue of the Earl of Belfast, by Patrick McDowell, is now in the City Hall; its pedestal was designed by Charles Lanyon; *The Builder*, 1855, p. 542. The Cooke statue is by S. F. Lynn; Brett, *Belfast*, p. 48.

**Pages 32 and 33**. Fisherwick Place and Great Victoria Street    C 1247   R 3859
1.  *Dublin Penny Journal*, supplement to first volume, 1832-3; Brett, *Belfast*, p. 19.
2.  *Irish Builder*, 1905, p. 406.

**Pages 34 and 35**. Grand Opera House and Hippodrome    I 321   R 8383
1.  See Robert McKinstry, 'The Grand Opera House, Belfast: restoring a Matcham theatre for today's audiences and actors' in B. M. Walker (ed.), *Frank Matcham, Theatre architect* (Belfast, 1980), pp 95-118.
2.  *Belfast directory*, 1909, p. 114.

**Page 36** The G.N.R. Station, Great Victoria Street    R 3861
1.  R. G. Morton, *Standard gauge railways in the North of Ireland* (Belfast, 1962), pp 9-10 and 22-3.
2.  Brett, *Belfast*, p. 27.

**Page 37**. Kensington Hotel, College Square East    R 10095
1.  *Belfast directory*, 1914, p. 276.
2.  *Belfast Telegraph*, 5 Sept 1978.

**Page 38**. Ulster Hall (Interior)    R 2387.
1.  Dunlop, *Barre* pp 22-4; Brett, *Belfast*, p. 32.

**Page 39**. Ulster Hall, Bedford Street    R 2388    C 1262
1.  *The Builder*, 1861, p. 211; *Dublin Builder*, 1861, p. 268 and 1862, p. 122.

**Pages 40 and 41**. Shaftesbury Square    R 316    R 314
1.  *Belfast Telegraph*, 14 Feb. 1941.
2.  S. T. Carleton, 'The growth of South Belfast' (M.A. thesis, 1967, The Queen's University, Belfast), pp 136 and 104 (hereafter cited as Carleton, *South Belfast*).
3.  *Belfast Newsletter*, 8 Oct. 1932.
4.  W. S. Leathem, *A history of the Church of Ireland in St Mary Magdalene parish, Belfast* (Belfast, 1939), pp 48-9.

**Page 42**. Deaf and Dumb Institute, Lisburn Road    R 3854
1.  Brett, *Belfast*, pp 25-6
2.  J. Kinghan in *Quarterly Review of Deaf-Mute Education*, Jan.-Apr. 1891, pp 4-9.

**Page 43**. Presbyterian College, College Park    C 2414
1.  *The Builder*, 1852, p. 495; for College's use by N. I. Parliament see *Irish Builder*, 1921, p. 549.

**Page 44**. Queen's College, University Road    I 1319
1.  J. C. Beckett and T. W. Moody, *Queen's Belfast, 1845-1949: the history of a university* (London, 1959), i, pp 103-115 (hereafter cited as Beckett and Moody, *Queen's Belfast*); Hugh Dixon and David Evans, *Historic buildings . . . in the vicinity of Queen's University* (Belfast, revised edition, 1975), pp 19-21 (hereafter cited as Dixon and Evans, *Historic Buildings . . . Queen's*).
2.  *Belfast Newsletter*, 12 Aug. 1849.

3.   Dixon, *Introduction*, p. 58.

**Page 45**. Hamilton Tower, Queen's College        R 10096
1.   Beckett and Moody, *Queen's Belfast*, pp362-3; *The Builder*, 1901, p. 421.
2.   Dixon and Evans, *Historic buildings . . . . Queen's*, pp 21-22.

**Page 46** Methodist College, College Gardens        NS 2430
1.   *Dublin Builder*, 1865, p. 208; *Irish Builder*, 1869, p. 9. Dixon and Evans, *Historic buildings . . . . Queen's*, p. 31.

**Page 47** Botanic Gardens Entrance        R 310
1.   McCracken, *Palm House*, pp 48-9; *Irish Builder*, 1879, p. 100.
2.   Carleton, *South Belfast*, p. 125; Dixon and Evans, *Historic buildings . . . . Queen's*, p. 37.

**Page 48** The Palm House, Botanic Gardens        R 2380
1.   McCracken, *Palm House*, pp 36-43. *. . . Queen's*, pp 31-3.
2.   Dixon and Evans, *Historic buildings . . . . Queen's*, pp 31-3.

**Page 49** Belfast Boat Club House, Stranmillis        R 2821
1.   *Belfast Boat Club: the first 100 years* (Belfast, 1976).

**Page 50** Fisherwick Presbyterian Church        R 8389
1.   Dixon and Evans, *Historic buildings . . . . Queen's*, p. 39.
2.   Carleton, *South Belfast*, p. 125.

**Page 51** St. Brigid's Catholic Church R8381
1.   Information from Canon Michael Dallat.

**Page 52** Ormeau Park        R 3416
1.   *Irish Penny Journal*, 1841, p. 377; and see W. A. Maguire in Beckett, *Belfast*, pp 33-6.
2.   W. A. Maguire, 'Ormeau House' in *Ulster Journal of Archaeology*, 3rd series, vol. 42, 1979, pp 66-71.
3.   Esler, *Belfast*, p. 52.

**Page 53** Ballynafeigh Methodist Church, Ormeau Road        R 6726
1.   Brett, *Belfast*, p. 52.
**Page 54** Dunville Park        R 8989
1.   *The Architect*, 1891, p. 104; *Belfast directory*, 1910, p. 103. A ranger's lodge was designed by W. H. Lynn; McLaughlin and Harvey papers, PRONI, D1898/1/13.

**Page 55** Royal Victoria Hospital        R 8976
1.   *Irish Builder*, 1899, p. 156; and R. S. Alison, *The seeds of time, being a short history of the Belfast General and Royal Hospital 1850-1903* (Belfast, 1977) pp 45-7.

**Page 56** St Peter's Catholic Pro-Cathedral        R 6724
1.   James O'Laverty, *An historical account of the diocese of Down and Connor*, (Dublin, 1880), ii pp 407-8 and 427-30 (hereafter cited as O'Laverty, *Down and Connor*); *Dublin Builder*, 1866, p. 253; *The Builder*, 1866, p. 745.
2.   Brett, *Belfast*, p. 36.

**Page 57** Falls Park, Falls Road        R 3412
1.   *Belfast Directory*, 1910, p. 103. Falls cemetery was designed by Gay and Swallow of Bradford; *The Builder*, 1867, p. 580. Milltown cemetery entrance was designed by Timothy Hevey; *Irish Builder*, 1870, p. 110.

**Pages 58 and 59** St Mary's College and St Dominic's College R 8377 R 8376
1.   Information from Canon Michael Dallat.

2.   *Belfast Morning News*, 1 May 1868.

**Pages 60 and 61** Provincial Bank and Royal Avenue        C 1264        R 2830
1.   Dunlop, *Barre*; Brett, *Belfast*, p. 34.
2.   *Irish Builder*, 1867, p. 316, and 1869, p. 6.
3.   *Irish Builder*, 1883, p. 30; *The Architect*, 1885, p. 58.

**Page 62** Royal Avenue and Castle Junction        R 2831
1.   Emrys Jones, *A social geography of Belfast* (Oxford, 1960), p. 57 (hereafter cited as Jones, *Belfast*)
2.   D. B. McNeill, *Ulster tramways and light railways* (Belfast, 1950), p. 13.

**Page 63** Royal Avenue        NS 1904
1.   *Irish Builder*, 1883, p. 43

**Page 64** Grand Central Hotel, Royal Avenue        I 2964
1.   *The Architect*, 1891, p. 168; Sir Frederick Bramwell was to have been engineer for the railway.
2.   A similar scheme for a Central Station in Donegall Square had been designed by John Lanyon; *Irish Builder*, 1873, p. 148.

**Page 65** Drawing Room, Grand Central Hotel        NS 2745
1.   *Handbook for the Grand Central Hotel, Belfast* (Belfast, 1911), (available in Belfast Central Library).

**Page 66** General Post Office, Royal Avenue        R 328
1.   Brett, *Belfast*, p. 50.
2.   *Irish Builder*, 1882, p. 351; *The Architect*, 1890, supplement p. 1.
3.   *The Builder*, 1909, p. 475.

**Page 67** Royal Avenue        I 2228
1.   Designed by Thomas Jackson; *Irish Builder*, 1884, p. 19; Brett, *Belfast*, p. 45.
2.   *Irish Builder*, 1886, p. 44, and 1888, p. 159.
3.   *Irish Builder*, 1886, p. 200.

**Page 68** York Street at junction with Royal Avenue        R 317
1.   Part of Gallagher's was designed by Samuel Stevenson in 1906; McLaughlin and Harvey papers, PRONI, D1898/1/30. For the damage to York Street Mill see *Bombs on Belfast* (Belfast, 1941), unpaginated (turn 11).

**Page 69** St Anne's Church and Cathedral        R 3855        R 8388
1.   Brett, *Belfast*, pp 4-5.
2.   *Irish Builder*, 1899, p. 114, and 1900, p. 439. For previous cathedral design by Lanyon and Lynn see *Ecclesiologist*, 1862, p. 340, and *The Builder*, 1863, p. 17.
3.   Brett, *Belfast*, p. 57.

**Pages 70 and 71**. York Street        I 330        I 339

**Pages 72 and 73**. Belfast and Northern Counties Railway Station R 2430        R 3858
1.   W. A. McCutcheon, *The industrial archaeology of Northern Ireland* (Belfast, 1980), pp 165-6; many records seem to have been lost in the blitz; see *Bombs on Belfast* (Belfast, 1941), unpaginated (turn 12-13).
2.   *Belfast directory*, 1909, p. 714

**Page 74**. St Patrick's Catholic Church        I 508
1.   O'Laverty, *Down and Connor*, ii, p. 422; Brett, *Belfast*, p. 41.
2.   O'Laverty, *Down and Connor*, ii, p. 419; Brett, *Belfast*, pp 11-12.

3. Datestone, and see Stephen Curwell, 'Early Gothic revival in Belfast' (unpublished paper, Department of Architecture, The Queen's University, Belfast).

**Page 75**. Victoria Barracks, North Queen Street      R 2390
1. *Belfast directory*, 1909, p. 79.

**Page 76**. Clifton Street      R 3841
1. The sculptor was C. B. Birch; Brett, *Belfast*, p. 48.
2. *Irish Builder*, 1887, p. 189; 1889, p. 280; and 1891, p. 229.
3. Brett, *Belfast*, pp 46-7.

**Page 77**. Carlisle Circus and Clifton Street      I 2673
1. *Irish Builder*, 1872, p. 170; Brett, *Belfast*, p. 45.
2. *Irish Builder*, 1874, p. 348; Brett, *Belfast*, p. 42.
3. See the different lamp beside the Hanna statue in the view opposite.
4. Harry Hems the sculptor was extremely thorough: 'stirrups, saddle cloth and pistol holsters have been taken from castings of the originals . . . . the sword is a facsimile of that wielded . . . . at the Battle of the Boyne'; *Irish Builder*, 1889, p. 280.

**Page 78**. Mater Infirmorum Hospital, Crumlin Road      I 2085.
1. *The Builder*, 1900, p. 451; *Belfast directory*, 1909, p. 82.

**Page 79**. Belfast Royal Academy      R 3857
1. *Irish Builder*, 1880, p. 114; Dixon, *1800-1900, p. 23*.

**Page 80**. Duncairn Gardens      R 9865
1. Jones, *Belfast*, pp 247-9.
2. P. G. Cleary, 'Spatial expansion and urban ecological change in Belfast with special reference to the role of local transportation, 1861-1917' (Ph.D. thesis, 1979, The Queen's University, Belfast), ii, p. 310.
3. Ibid., p. 600-3; Jones, *Belfast, pp 52-3*.

**Page 81**. Steam Tram on the Antrim Road      C 2408
1. *Gone but not forgotten: Belfast trams, 1872-1954* (Belfast, 1979; second edition, 1980), pp 8-9; Patrick Flanagan, *Transport in Ireland* (Dublin, 1969), p. 74.

**Page 82**. Jubilee Avenue at the entrance to Alexandra Park      R 3863

**Page 83**. Alexandra Park      R3866
1. *Belfast directory*, 1910, p. 102.

**Page 84**. Cave Hill Road      I 1992

**Page 85**. Entrance Gates to Fortwilliam Park      C 2400      C 2402
1. Brett, *Belfast*, p. 33; for even earlier photograph see Dunlop, *Barre*.

**Page 86**. Belfast Castle      C 2405
1. W. A. Maguire in Beckett, *Belfast*, pp 37-9.
2. *The Architect*, 1873, p. 214.
3. *Belfast directory*, 1910, p. 84.
4. Brenda Collins, 'The Edwardian city', in Beckett, *Belfast*, p. 171.

**Page 87** Cave Hill      R 9869
1. Alice Milligan, *Hero lays* (Dublin, 1908), p. 32.

**Page 90**. Harbour Office      R 8193
1. See Robin Sweetnam, 'The development of the port' in Beckett, *Belfast*, pp 57-77 (hereafter cited as Sweetnam, *The port*); D. J. Owen, *A short history of the port of Belfast*, (Belfast, 1917), pp 33-47 (hereafter cited as Owen, *Belfast port*).

2. Brett, *Belfast*, p. 29; Smith, little known as an architect, also designed the Calder Fountain beside the Custom House; *Dublin Builder*, 1859, p. 62.
3. *Irish Builder*, 1890, p. 295; McLaughlin and Harvey papers, PRONI, D.1898/1/5.

**Page 91**. Clarendon Dock      C 2526
1. Owen, *Belfast port*, p. 39.
2. *Belfast Examiner*, 20 Feb. and 12 Aug. 1879; Brett, *Belfast*, p. 41.

**Page 92**. The Custom House      C 1253
1. *Annual statement of trade of the United Kingdom for 1905, vol. II*, 26-28 [Cd 3022], H. C. 1906, CXViii, 38-40.
2. *24th Report from the Board of Public Works, Ireland, p. 26, H.C. 1856 (2140) XIX, 382*.

**Page 93**. Spencer Dock      R 4742
1. Owen, *Belfast port*, pp 41 and 76.
2. D. B. McNeill, *Irish passenger steamship services: vol. 1, north of Ireland* (Newton Abbot, 1969), pp 142-3 (hereafter cited as McNeill, *Irish steamships*).

**Pages 94 and 95**. Queen's Bridge—left view      C 2423      right view I 640
1. J. P. Lawson, *Gazetteer of Ireland*, 1842, p. 149.
2. *Irish Builder*, 1885, p. 70; Brett, *Belfast*, p. 24

**Page 96**. River View      R 4745
1. Owen, *Belfast port*, p. 39.

**Page 97**. Queen's Quay and Railway Station      C 2438
1. *The Architect*, 1892, supplement p. 11.
2. *Census of Ireland, 1901: vol. III, province of Ulster*, 17 [Cd 1123], H.C. 1902, CXXVi, 205 (hereafter cited as *Ulster census, 1901*).

**Page 98**. Queen's Quay      NS 2530
1. Ian Wilson, *John Kelly Ltd: an history* (n.d. leaflet in Linen Hall Library), pp 4-5.

**Page 99**. Discharging coal, Queen's Quay      NS 2537
1. Information from *Lloyd's Registers of Shipping* (various dates).

**Pages 100 and 101**. P.S. Adder      R2824      S.S. Viper      NS 1695
1. McNeill, *Irish steamships*, p. 43.

**Pages 102 and 103**. Bangor Boat Terminus      NS 1769      Steamer      C 2444
1. Ibid, pp 137-48
2. Ibid, p. 147
3. This song was kindly provided by Dr P. G. Cleary.

**Pages 104 and 105**. Jetty NS 2448      Slieve Bernagh      R 8980
1. McNeill, Irish steamships, pp 147-52.

**Page 108**. Brookfield Mill, Crumlin Road      R 2413
1. Emily Boyle, ' Linenopolis : the rise of the textile industry ', in Beckett, *Belfast*, p. 47 (hereafter cited as Boyle, *Linenopolis*).
2. Jonathan Bardon, *Belfast: an illustrated history* (Belfast, 1982), p. 262 (hereafter cited as Bardon, *Belfast*).

**Page 109**. Interior of Ewart's Mill, Crumlin Road      R 2411
1. See Boyle, *Linenopolis*, pp 51-3.
2. This may be the new flax spinning mill built for William Ewart and Son reported in *Dublin Builder*, 1865, p. 228.

**Page 110**. Reeling room in Ewart's Mill, Crumlin Road    R 2410
1.  See B. M. Walker, *Shadows on glass* (Belfast, 1976). This information on wages and prices came originally from Dr Emily Boyle.

**Page 111**. York Street Mill    R 2412
1.  Moore, *Belfast guide*, pp 90-2.
2.  *Ulster census, 1901*, 21 and 30, 209 and 218.
3.  Noel Nesbitt, *The changing face of Belfast* (Belfast 1969; second revised edition, 1982), p. 43.

**Page 112**. Weaving room in linen factory    NS 2508

**Page 113**. Linen Bleach Green    R 2415
1.  For further information see Moore, *Belfast guide*, pp 87-95.

**Page 114**. Royal Ulster Works    C 2407
1.  Diane Gracey, 'The decline and fall of Marcus Ward' in *Irish Booklore*, I, no. 2 (Aug. 1971) p. 187.

**Page 115**. Bedford Street    R 3844
1.  *Guide to Belfast, 1902* (London, 1902) p. 28.
2.  *Irish Builder*, 1869, p. 213.
3.  Information on the subject and other aspects of the linen business was kindly provided by Mr. Edwin Bryson.

**Pages 116 and 117**. Albert Bridge    R 3862    Queen's Bridge    C 5072
1.  *Irish Builder*, 1890, p. 209; the fine ironwork was by Messrs Handyside of Derby.
2.  Brett, *Belfast*, p. 51.
3.  *Belfast directory,* 1909, p. 91

**Page 118**. Pilot Office    R 2383
1.  *Shipbuilding: development of iron and steel shipbuilding in Belfast* (undated leaflet, published by the Ulster Folk and Transport Museum).
2.  Owen, *Belfast port*, pp 55-6.

**Page 119**. Ferry Boat at the quays    R 4743
.1  D. B. McNeill, *Coastal passenger steamers and inland navigations in the north of Ireland* (Belfast, 1960; 2nd impression 1967), p. 11.
2.  Owen, *Belfast port*, p. 81.
3.  McNeill, *Irish steamships*, pp 78 and 216.

**Pages 120 and 121**. Queen's Shipyard    R 9240    R 9241
1.  Owen, *Belfast port*, pp 52-5.
2.  *Lloyd's Registers of Shipping*.

**Page 122**. Tug in dock    R 2823
1.  Owen, *Belfast harbour, pp 45 and 78-9.*

**Page 123**. No. 1 Jetty, Abercorn Basin    R 9258
1.  Lawrence Dunn, *Famous liners of the past, Belfast built* (London, 1964), p. 136 (hereafter cited as Dunn, *Liners*).

**Page 124**. S. S. Teutonic    C 5078
1.  Dunn, *Liners*, p. 192

**Page 125**. Alexandra Graving Dock    R 1663
1.  *Irish Builder*, 1892, p. 247; Brett, *Belfast*, p. 50
2.  Bardon, *Belfast*, p. 130.
3.  *Daily Mail*, 25 July 1939. We are grateful for this information to Mr Michael Villiers-Stuart, who served as a crew hand on the barque *Pommern* which left Belfast in September 1938 for Australia.

**Page 126**  Falls Road Park R3410.

# ACKNOWLEDGEMENTS

The authors wish to thank all who have helped with the production of this book. Special thanks are due to the Trustees of the National Library of Ireland for permission to reproduce the photographs from the Lawrence Collection. The photographic department of the Library kindly provided the prints for publication.

We also gratefully acknowledge help from Belfast Central Library; the Linen Hall Library; The Queen's University Library; the Public Record Office of Northern Ireland; the Historic Monuments and Buildings Branch, DoENI; Dr W. A. Maguire and Mr Noel Nesbitt of the Ulster Museum; Mr John Moore and Mr Michael McCaughan of the Ulster Folk and Transport Museum; Mr John Erskine and Miss Carol Doherty of Stranmillis College Library; Professor Alistair Rowan for permission to use material from *The Buildings of Ireland* archive; Mr Edwin Bryson; Dr P. G. Cleary; Canon Michael Dallat; Mr Wesley McCann; Father Ambrose Macauley; Mr Anthony Merrick; Mr Robin Sweetnam; Canon W. G. L. Walker, and Dr Christopher Woods.

Finally we wish to thank the late George Birmingham for providing the epigraph; and the trustees of his estate and his publishers Messrs William Heinemann Ltd for permission to take this quotation from his autobiography *Pleasant places*.

# INDEX

*Bold type denotes plate titles*